TWICKENHAM
PAST

Part of a 'A View of Twickenham' by Edward Ironside 1786.

TWICKENHAM PAST

A Visual History
of Twickenham
and Whitton

Edited by
Donald Simpson

HISTORICAL PUBLICATIONS

First published 1993
by Historical Publications Ltd
32 Ellington Street, London N7 8PL
(Tel: 0171-607 1628)
Reprinted 1998

ISBN 0 948667 22 2

Typeset by Historical Publications Ltd
Printed and bound by South China Printing Company,
Hong Kong/China

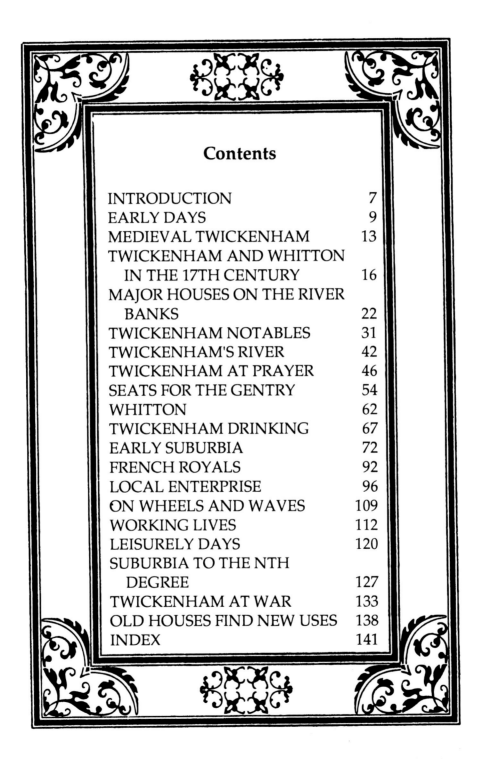

Contents

The Illustrations

The following have kindly given their permission to use illustrations:

The London Borough of Richmond upon Thames: frontispiece, 77, 81, 100, 101, 105, 127, 129, 131, 137, 140, 142, 144, 169, 173, 180, 191, 196
Bamber Gascoigne from his book *Images of Twickenham* (1981): 1, 2, 3, 28, 30, 31, 33, 34, 36, 37, 41, 42, 45, 46, 67, 71, 82, 83, 87, 89, 90, 96, 97, 103, 108, 110, 111, 112, 113, 115, 118, 119, 120, 121, 123, 124, 125, 126, 133, 134, 177, 178
Bodleian Library: Oxford, 23
British Museum: 9, 13
National Maritime Museum: 58
National Portrait Gallery: 52
Royal Institute of British Architects: 92
St Mary's Church, Twickenham: 11, 16, 48, 49, 60, 80
Sir John Soane's Museum: 109
Trafalgar School: 153
Victoria and Albert Museum: 88
Wallace Collection: 63
Mrs M. Alford: 170
John Boys: 187
Miss M. Brown: 190
Martin Fenton: 104, 163, 164, 168, 183, 184, 185
Miss M. Groves: 179
Ron Killick: 171
Mrs J. King: 146
Miss Joan Pearce: 154
Mrs Pam Post: 186
Henry Potts: 117
Rafael Valls: jacket
D.H. Simpson: 12, 21, 24, 25, 26, 32, 38, 39, 43, 44, 47, 50, 51, 54, 55, 56, 57, 59, 61, 62, 66, 68, 70, 79, 94, 98, 99, 107, 122, 132, 145, 147, 188, 194

A.C.B. Urwin: 4, 5, 6, 8, 10, 14, 15, 17, 18, 19, 20, 27, 40, 65, 69, 84, 85, 91, 102, 106, 114, 116, 138, 148, 149, 150, 151, 156, 157, 158, 159, 165, 166, 167, 175, 176, 181, 182, 195
Dr T.H.R. Cashmore: 53, 64, 72, 95, 128, 135, 136, 139, 155, 193,
V.Rosewarne, 22, 130, 160, 161, 162, 192

The *jacket illustration* is an oil painting of Twickenham in about 1760 by Samuel Scott (1710?-72). It shows the group of houses in Riverside which still survive, including the (White) Swan Inn. Ferryside is on the right. The tower of St Mary's church can be seen beyond the barge on the left.
The *montage* reproduced on the half-title page is taken from a poster devised by Patricia Astley-Cooper for an exhibition in the Orleans Gallery in 1981, organised in conjunction with the Borough of Twickenham Local History Society, entitled *Twickenham 1600-1900: People and Places.* The individuals shown are:
Rear: Lady Mary Wortley Montagu; Kitty Clive; the three Ladies Waldegrave; Lord Mendip; Lady Di Beauclerk; the Earl of Shelburne; the Earl of Clarendon.
Second Row: Lady Hobhouse; Horace Walpole; the Earl of Rochester; Paul Whitehead; King Louis Philippe; the Countess of Bedford; Sir Benjamin Hobhouse.
Front: Henrietta Howard, Countess of Suffolk; Sir Thomas Nott; Sir John Hawkins; Hannah Pritchard; John Cam Hobhouse; Richard Owen Cambridge; Alexander Pope.

Introduction

The people of Twickenham have long been interested in their own history. The first resident to compile a *History of Twickenham* was Edward Ironside, a servant of the East India Company, who lived firstly at 6 Sion Row and later in King Street. He produced his book in 1797, though there is evidence that parts at least were written more than a decade earlier. He was also sufficiently interested, and artistic, to leave us the first detailed and accurate watercolour of the Twickenham riverside at that time, which was found in his personal and annotated copy of his book in a London bookshop in 1964.

However, he had been beaten to the post by the Rev. Daniel Lysons, A.M., F.A.S., who dealt with Twickenham in the third volume of *The Environs of London being an Historical Account of the Towns, Villages and Hamlets within Twelve Miles of the Capital* which he published in 1795.

The third major book in the written record of Twickenham history was *Memorials of Twickenham* published in 1872, by the Rev. R.S. Cobbett, Curate of St Mary's Church. Though not free from blemishes, it did much to correct the errors of his predecessors, and is still a valued source, despite the limitations, such as the concentration on the great names and lack of social background, of the style of historical writing of the time.

In the latter part of the nineteenth century the literary world of the eighteenth century, many of whose luminaries lived in Twickenham and neighbouring towns, attracted such literary/historical essayists as Henry Austin Dobson, and a volume by a local author in the same tradition is F.C. Hodgson's *Thames-side in the past; Sketches of its Literature & Society*, published in 1913 and dedicated to Dr J.R. Leeson, later Twickenham's Charter Mayor.

A noted figure in local history was that of Arthur Burrell (1859-1946), who had been headmaster of Borough Road College, Isleworth, from 1899 to 1912 and was an effective and in some ways formidable Chairman of the Twickenham Library Committee from 1926 to 1944. He placed later historians in his debt by compiling the massive *Book of Twickenham* containing photographs of significant documents in a wide variety of collections relating to Twickenham's past, for which he was created a Freeman of Twickenham in 1938; he lectured extensively to schools and adult organisations, but never wrote a book on his favourite subject.

By the middle of the 20th century more properly researched and detailed history began to appear in the series of the Victoria County Histories. The third volume of *A History of the County of Middlesex*, published in 1962, has a chapter by Susan Reynolds dealing with Twickenham in detail: this gives full references and must be regarded as the starting point of modern Twickenham History.

The first volume of a short-lived series *A New Survey of England*, the admirable *Middlesex* by Michael Robbins, was published in 1953. Mr Robbins addressed one of the planning meetings of a provisional committee set up by Twickenham's York House Society in 1961 to organise a local history society. In April 1962 the Borough of Twickenham Local History Society (a name reflecting its involvement in the then Borough of Twickenham, which included Teddington and the Hamptons as well as Twickenham and Whitton) was set up. In 1965 it began publishing its series of Papers, two or three of which have followed annually;' the latest is number 68. It has also published Occasional Papers, two being leaflets designed to help local researchers, the other two longer volumes, *Alexander Pope's Twickenham*, and *York House*. The Society has also prepared two volumes of photographs, *Twickenham as it was* and *Bygone Twickenham*.

Following the success of his *Images of Richmond* in 1978, Bamber Gascoigne compiled, with Jonathan Ditchburn, a companion volume *Images of Twickenham with Hampton and Teddington*, published in 1981, in which he acknowledges the assistance of 'a quartet of devoted and well-informed sleuths' from the Local History Society in preparing the text. We in turn are indebted to him for the use of a substantial number of photographs of prints used in his book.

In addition, numerous books and booklets have appeared on individuals, events and places in the locality, and local literary figures such as Pope, Lady Mary Wortley Montagu, and Horace Walpole have been the subject of scholarly biographies and editions of letters and writings, most notably the Yale edition of Horace Walpole's letters in 48 volumes.

This volume is concerned only with Twickenham and Whitton, the historic Parish of Twickenham. There is so much detailed history of the area available that it can include no more than an outline of some aspects of its history, together with some episodes and anecdotes which lend themselves to this treatment and to illustration. It has been written by members of the BOTLHS, notably Alan Urwin (without whose initiative we should never have started), Dick Cashmore, Brian Pearce, Vic Rosewarne and myself, with contributions from Helen McCutcheon Nelson (schools) and Paul Barnfield (non-conformity). Final editing and arrangement have been my responsibility. We have freely availed ourselves of the writings already published by the Society, and hope that those whose researches we have plundered will accept this general acknowledgement. These publications comprise nearly 2,500 pages, with many relevant illustrations, and in addition to the older works mentioned above may be consulted in the Local History Collection in Twickenham.

Many illustrations in this volume have been suggested or provided by the authors, or obtained from organisations to which we are greatly indebted for their permission to use them, particularly the Local Studies section of the Richmond upon Thames Libraries, whose staff, under the leadership of Diana Howard, have been very good friends to all local historical researchers.

Donald Simpson

1. A Prospect of Richmond in Surry. Engraving of 1726 showing Twickenham, very little developed, to the rear.

Early Days

Very little can be written on the long period before the Norman Conquest. Up to AD704 the only information about our past has been the result of pure luck - chance finds when digging drains and the foundations of houses, in the cultivation of market and private gardens, and one exercise in serious archaeological excavation in one of the few open spaces in the centre of Twickenham available to allow this. One must thank the individuals who noted what they saw and then kept the bones and flints and arrow and javelin heads and pieces of ceramics, etc., that the spade turned up. Some of them gave their finds to the Library (and now to the Orleans House Gallery which is collecting them for a Museum of Twickenham) to be indexed for future research.

After AD704, when kingdoms and kings and the Church and bishops appear, from charters and wills the information we call History begins to outline the earliest stage of our community. Then William I, the Conqueror, in 1086 ordered and organised the fantastically detailed Domesday Book survey of almost the whole country. From this the first estimate of Twickenham's population and area can be made.

2. A View from Richmond Hill up the River. Engraving of 1749; in the centre is Orleans House, to the right Marble Hill House, and above the trees can be seen the Church tower.

3. *A Perspective View of Twickenham. Engraving of 1749 by Rooker after A. Heckell. The Earl of Strafford's house is the large building with central pediment to the right; the Church can be seen on the left.*

PREHISTORY

Twickenham, as everywhere else in England, has been influenced by the country's attachment to and then separation from the Continent, and by the four successive ice ages, with the long alternating hot and cold periods. These factors have engineered the local landscape and provided its two rivers, the Thames and the Crane. The last ice cap only came as far as St Albans, but it was this period that provided the first evidence that we have of the local flora and fauna; we have no evidence of Man then. Even in the 2000 years since the Romans first arrived, there has been continual geological change; south-east England has sunk, and tides that once only reached London Bridge now reach upstream, and require that east Twickenham be protected by flood walls.

The bones illustrated here were found in 1892, when main drainage was being installed in Pope's Grove to replace cesspits and soakaways. At a depth of 18 feet a layer of 2-3 feet-thick slimy river mud was found, coarse and loamy in places, and under a thick layer of dark blue and grey gravel. It was rich in animal and vegetable matter, and about 3,000 mammalian bones, of bison, wild ox, row deer, reindeer, wild boar and wolf were found, but there were no flint tools to indicate the presence of Man.

In 1956 the same stratum was recognised in Willment's pit where gravel and sand were extracted next to the South Middlesex Hospital and today's

4. *Bones found in 1892 during laying of sewers.*

Tesco supermarket. In this layer the same animal bones were found as in 1892, also those of mammoth and woolly rhinoceros. They were dated as around 41,000 BC, in the middle of a warmer period during the last Ice Age. Remains of 225 named species of beetles still found in Britain today were also identified and from these the nature of the landscape and its flora could be conjectured. Despite the fact that the climate was no colder then than in the same area today there was an absence of trees. This was probably the result of a tundra-like climate immediately preceding and lasting perhaps as long as 15,000 years and too hostile to support tree growth.

The riverbed between Eel Pie Island and Twickenham has produced other finds - flint flakes, neolithic implements, axes, horn hoes and hammers and the remains of a pile causeway from the mainland to the island.

The first evidence of Man in Twickenham, pottery and flints, was found in a Church Street car park dig, organised by the Local History Society, in 1966, and dated as 3,000 BC.

SAXON TIMES

In AD704 a grant of land mentions Twickenham (spelt 'Twicanhom'): 'on the east and south it is terminated by the River Thames, on the north by a flooded plain, the name of which is Fishbourne [the area of the river Crane and Birkett's Brook]...'

Following this there were later deeds and a variety of spellings of the name. There can be no certainty as to its origin. 'Ham' was a Saxon name ending, and there is also a Saxon word 'wic' derived from a Roman word 'vicus' for a small settlement. However, there is another word, 'hamm', of a different and perhaps English origin, meaning 'land in a river bend or promontory, dry ground in a marsh, river meadow...' This is much more likely, as Twickenham lies between the rivers Thames and Crane, and the land beyond the Crane was marshy even as late as the 16th century. A link with a personal name 'Twicca' has also been suggested, but is not confirmed by documentation.

TWICKENHAM IN 1086: THE DOMESDAY BOOK

William the Conqueror gave the manor comprising Twickenham, Whitton, Isleworth and Hounslow to Walter de St Valery, a kinsman who had come with him from Normandy. Twickenham and Whitton were not separately mentioned in the Domesday Book of 1086, but it is estimated that they formed about a quarter of the total manor, with a population of about 25 households in Twickenham and five in Whitton, occupying about 2,355 acres of which less than one half was farmed in large open fields. These open fields were South Field, lying between Cross Deep and the Hampton Road, and the Town Field, between Twickenham and Whitton.

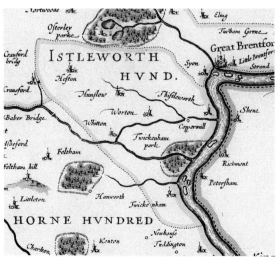

5. Map of Isleworth Hundred and surrounding areas from John Blaeu Atlas Novus, *1648.*

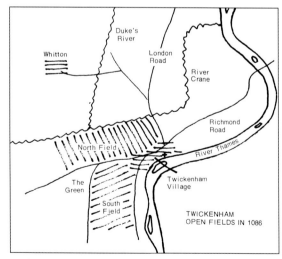

6. Sketch map of Twickenham from the evidence of the Domesday Book.

7. *Aerial view of Twickenham and Eel Pie Island.*

Medieval Twickenham

With peace and Norman organisation, the population began to increase and unused land was taken into cultivation by the opening of new common fields divided into strips. In 1219 there is the first mention of Whitton when 25 acres were granted to Radulfus, son of Gilbert of Whitton. After this come the names of hundreds of fields, closes, furlongs, crofts, warrens, groves, meadows and heaths. A family name that has appeared consistently since - York - appears in 1381.

TWICKENHAM PARK

The largest enclosure was made in 1227 when Henry III gave his 18-year-old brother, Richard, newly-created Earl of Cornwall, the manor of Isleworth. A manor house was built in what is now Lower Square, Isleworth, a stone hall with basement and kitchen, and a chapel with king's and queen's chambers, all surrounded by a moat; outside were several granges, granaries and barns. Richard also enclosed within a double ditch and hedge the pear-shaped Park, stretching from the mouth of the Crane to the point where Richmond Bridge was built in 1777 (the line of today's Richmond and St Margaret's Roads and the River Thames). Inside the fence, or pale, cattle were kept and trees for both building and fuel. He also built, *c*1240, a rabbit warren at the southern end of the Park near Richmond Road. Rabbits, brought over to

England by the Normans, were bred not only for their delicate meat, but for their availability in winter; their skins also provided winter clothing and bed covering.

Twickenham Park was briefly the site of the Monastery of St Saviour and St Bridget of Syon, founded by Henry V. Established here in 1415, it was found that the location was unhealthy, despite the digging of a drainage ditch - this is now a long, narrow, ornamental lake within the communal lands of the St Margaret's estate. A new monastery was therefore built in what is now Syon Park and the inmates of the

8. Richard Earl of Cornwall (left) greeting the Sultan of Arak.

9. (Top right) Seal of Richard, Earl of Cornwall.

10. (Bottom right) Twicknam Parke House 1607, from the map by Ralph Treswell.

Twickenham building moved there. Though Syon monastery was dissolved in 1538 the nuns continued in the Low Countries and in Portugal and returned to England in 1831; their convent, now at South Brent in Devon, is thought to be the only Roman Catholic establishment in the country to have had a continuous existence since before the Reformation.

Once the monastery had left Twickenham Park the grounds were used for pleasure. About 1450 Queen Margaret of Anjou wrote to the keeper of Shene Park requesting him to keep at Twickenham Park 'for our disporte and recreacion, two or three of the greatest bukkes in my lords parc'. The fields nearby, but outside the Park, known as Ferry Mead and Moor Mead, were used to provide additional food for the deer in the Park.

A timber-framed hunting lodge was built in the area of today's Cassilis Road in 1375/7 - detailed accounts of the materials used for this are extant. It had a floor area in two storeys of 1,100 sq. feet, and cost £13.8.2d to build.

The first major house, timber-framed but with lower courses of brick, was built in 1561/2; it comprised about 4,000 sq. feet of floor space in two storeys. It was superseded by another brick house in 1608/9, only a year or so before the construction of Ham House across the river at Petersham. This building, Twickenham Park House, was occupied by the nobility and the wealthy until 1803, after which it was gradually demolished.

Originally, the park was known as Isleworth Park, and later as the New Park of Shene (from *c*1440), the New Park of Richmond (from *c*1504 when Shene had been renamed Richmond by Henry VII), and after 1592, when it came into private hands, as Twickenham Park. Today, however, when virtually the whole of its area has been built over, this name still appears on some large-scale maps, referring to the district be-

11. (Above) Release of 1443 from Matilda Abbess of Syon Monastery, now in St Mary's church, Twickenham.

12. (Top right) Lucy, Countess of Bedford, who lived at Twickenham Park 1608-18. Engraving by W. Freeman after Honthorst.

13. (Bottom right) Seal of Syon Monastery, 15th century.

14. Twickenham Park House, 1795; drawn and engraved by W. Angus

tween the railway and Richmond Road, while the northern half of the Park is now St Margaret's.

SETTING THE BOUNDARIES

When there was ample waste and uncultivated land, boundaries were of little importance but as enclosures became more frequent they became significant. In 1439 a dispute arose between Twickenham and Isleworth over the boundary from the Thames and across Twickenham Park to Ivy Bridge where the road crosses the Crane river. An arbitrator, Master John Somerseth, Chancellor of the King's Exchequer, and a jury of twelve men from both parishes, agreed a boundary and had it marked with 'stakes of tree and stones'. Many of these markers are noted on the 25" Ordnance Survey, but none can now be seen on the ground. It was also agreed that the respective vicars and their parishioners should periodically process along each side of the boundary.

As Edward Ironside recorded late in the 18th century, the 1609 Twickenham Park House 'standeth in two parishes of Twickenham and Isleworth. In the hall fronting the south west is laid on the mosaic pavement of black and white marble a small iron cross which divided the two parishes...when the parishioners in the course of beating the bounds...assembled in the hall, one of the leaders climbed through a window on the opposite side of the house...a prayer was offered by the priest. Refreshments were then given to all taking part in the

15. Boundary Mark of 1909 photographed by Alan Urwin.

ceremony, and they departed on their journey along the boundary.'

One of the last such processions took place in 1909. A concrete boundary stone, at the side of Duck's Walk, marks the point where the then boundary reached the river. Nearby another stone is marked IP/TP. Since then the two local authorities (now boroughs, not parishes) have agreed to simplify the collection of rates by moving the boundary to the north side of The Avenue, by Twickenham Bridge, which opened in 1933.

Twickenham and Whitton in the 17th Century

The first of the country houses that came to line the Twickenham riverside was built in Twickenham Park in 1561. By 1797, when Horace Walpole died, his Gothic Strawberry Hill completed the line upstream, and had founded an architectural style. Several other houses were built a little inland, and by 1720 other smaller houses began to appear, built and occupied by the rising middle classes, and some were even built by 'trade'.

In 1720 John Macky, a government agent and spy, described Twickenham as a 'Village remarkable for an abundance of curious seats' ('curious' then referred to the quality of things, exquisite, choice, deserving or exciting curiosity). By then, too, the 'quality' were well established. In 1722 Lady Mary Wortley Montagu wrote 'I am at Twickenham where there is at this time more company than in London' and 'Twickenham is become so fashionable, and the neighbourhood so enlarged, that it is more like Tunbridge or Bath than a country retreat'. Her friend, Alexander Pope, who had commissioned Kneller to paint her in Turkish costume, was one of the few residents who had made enough money (from his own writing, principally his translation of the *Iliad* into English verse) by his early twenties to afford his

own home and to have it improved in the Palladian style by the architect, James Gibbs (also designer of the Octagon in Twickenham).

In the milieu of Twickenham poets and painters found much scope and profit, beginning with John Donne in the early 1600s. A succession of painters and artists that followed produced work that enables us to see in considerable detail how Classical Twickenham looked in the 18th century.

By 1664 population had grown in Twickenham to about 1015 and in Whitton to 120 people, with 218 and 29 houses respectively. The Hearth Tax records of that period show an average of 4.1 hearths in each part of the parish, with eleven large houses containing between 15 and 37 hearths. The number of houses exempt from the tax because of poverty and their small size numbered 76 in Twickenham and 10 in Whitton.

TWICKENHAM VILLAGE IN 1635

Reproduced here are a section and details from the map of the area drawn by Moses Glover and completed in 1635. The Thames and Eel Pie Island are shown to the left. The basic street layout of today is shown, with other features:

Cross Deep is shown top left, leading towards Teddington: note that the 'deep' was '2 fadham'. Heath Road leads towards today's Green with the first houses on the Hampton Road and 'Heth-Rowe', and there are houses along the Staines Road.

South Field at the top of the map, lies between Cross Deep and Heath Road. The Towne or North Field is between Heath Road and the river. These were the first open fields which were divided into

16. Memorial of Francis Poulton, a distinguished lawyer who lived at the Grove (on the corner of Cross Deep) and died in 1642, and his wife Susannah. Photo by Robin Shotter.

17. Detail from Glover's map of 1635. The map includes the only picture, inadequate though it is, of the original St Mary's church. York House is shown under construction for Mr Pecarnes (or Pitcarne). Opposite is the three-gabled manor house in Church Street, occupied by Lady Walter, with its garden and park extending as far back as Amyand Park Road.

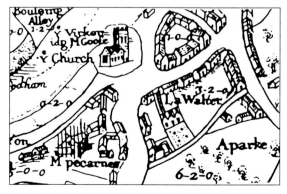

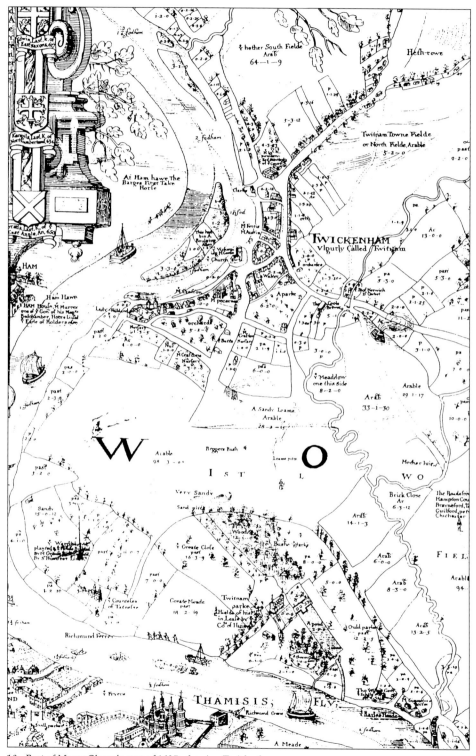

18. *Part of Moses Glover's map of 1635, showing Twickenham.*

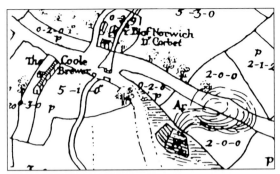

19. *Detail as above showing Brick Kiln and the Cole Brewery, later rebuilt on the site of the Bishop of Norwich's house.*

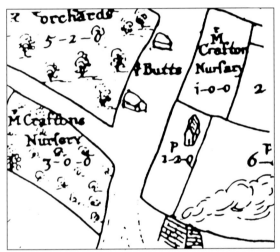

20. *The Butts, nurseries, and another brick kiln (detail from Glover)*

strips and allocated to the families in the village.

The river Crane may be seen to the right of the map, crossing the London Road beside today's railway station, and proceeding towards what is now St Margaret's.

Various fields, with their acreage, are noted to the north of the village; most of them are pastoral, but some are arable.

To the right of this map was the Monk's (now known as the Duke's) River, an artificial waterway bringing water from the river Colne. This was constructed to feed the mills at Syon House in the days when it was a monastery.

The house of Richard Corbet (1582-1635), Bishop of Norwich, beside the river Crane where Heatham House now stands.

Thomas Cole's brewery, beside today's railway station. The family later moved the brewery across the road to the site of the present Sorting Office and built Heatham House for themselves.

The making of bricks and tiles died out after the Romans left. Imports from Flanders began in the 13th century, but their manufacture and use here only really began in the 15th century. Richmond Palace was rebuilt using brick after it burnt down in 1497, and it was also used at Hampton Court. Twickenham began to produce bricks at this time. Glover's map of 1635 shows two brick kilns, and also brick 'closes', where clay was dug and bricks made - there were probably quite a number of each. Twickenham Park House was the first major building of brick in the area. Virtually all the early brick houses in Twickenham are of the standardised so-called 'Tudor' type, which continued to be used until the modern brick size was introduced in the later 18th century.

When the manor house in Church Street was demolished in 1934 its old 16th to 18th century bricks were utilised in repairs at Hampton Court Palace.

The Butts, the targets for archery practice or the mounds in front of which the targets were placed, are clearly marked towards the bottom of the map, on the edge of the village and the East Field. They were probably sited here before the days of the longbow of the late 14th century, and probably before the East Field was created between the village and the enclosure of Twickenham Park in 1227.

WHITTON IN THE 17TH CENTURY

Whitton is first mentioned around 1200 in a document listing assarts (land converted to arable use) from the heath, though it had probably been settled in the 10th or 11th centuries. By the 13th century Whitton's limits to the west were defined by the present Hounslow Road, High Street and Percy Road, the ancient line between Twickenham and Isleworth. The River Crane formed a natural southern boundary, the northern was Birkett's Brook, and the eastern was formed by that stretch of the Duke of Northumberland's river (constructed in 1545) between the Crane at Twickenham and north to Isleworth. These boundaries were confirmed with the founding of the new church of St Philip and St James in 1882.

The maps of Ralph Treswell (1607) and Moses Glover (1635) show Whitton as a hamlet centred on the crossroads where the present Nelson and Kneller Roads and Whitton Dean meet. Treswell's map shows a house in the occupation of royal courtier, Sir John Suckling, at the junction of the present Nelson and

21. *Sir John Suckling*

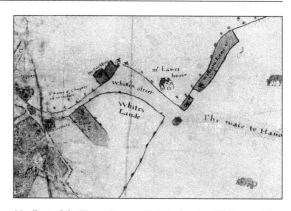

22. *Part of the Treswell map of 1607, showing Whitton, with Sir John Suckling's house at the top.*

present Kneller Hall. It was the fourth largest house in Twickenham parish, with twenty rooms.

In the reign of James II the summer scene at Whitton was enlivened by the encampments of the army on Hounslow Heath. On land in Whitton, leased from Lord Belasye, the king built a hospital, barn and stables. This land is now the site of Whitton School in Percy Road, and the events of those summers is now recalled by Hospital Bridge Road.

THE CIVIL WAR

Twickenham witnessed no fighting during the Civil War. Men were being drilled in the parish in the autumn of 1642, but the nearest conflict was the Battle of Brentford on 12 November of that year. The following day barges carrying cannon and troops from Kingston tried to pass down river to London but ran into trouble at Syon House where they came under fire from royalists lining the Middlesex bank. Some of the barges were sunk and the royalists 'took the rest, and 8 pieces [of cannon] in them, for our breakfast'.

In August 1647 the New Model Army, in difficulties with both Parliament and London, was concentrated around Brentford, Hounslow and Twickenham. At the same time, Charles I, a prisoner of the Army, was moved to Hampton Court. Fighting broke out again in 1648 and there was skirmishing around Surbiton and towards Kingston, in which the royalists were routed. The following year there were riots in Twickenham, some months after the execution of the king. An attempt was made to proclaim Charles II as king. The instigators were Sir Thomas Nott of Twickenham Park, who had fought as a colonel in the royalist army, and his wife, but they managed to save themselves by paying £1,500 to the Committee for Compounding.

Warren Roads. Made rich by his royal household posts, he had by 1635 built a much larger house incorporating a banqueting hall on the present Warren Road.

Sir John Suckling's eldest son, the celebrated Cavalier poet, also Sir John, was born at Whitton in 1609. He inherited his father's fortune, estimated at over £25,000 in 1627, and as a young man he travelled in Holland and Germany. On his return to England he threw himself excessively into the enjoyments of court life - gambling, reciting verses, playing bowls. He was elected to the Short Parliament but he fled the country in 1641 after implication in a plot to free the Earl of Strafford from the Tower. It is thought that Suckling, in Paris in reduced circumstances, committed suicide by taking poison at the age of thirty-two.

The Suckling house was later acquired by Lord Belasye, a prominent Catholic supporter of James II. According to Titus Oates he was to have been in command of a Catholic army which was in formation and in consequence of this scare-mongering Belasye and others were imprisoned in the Tower in 1678 and not released until 1684. The old house was demolished sometime before 1745.

Another important house was that built between 1635 and 1646 by Edmund Cooke, on the site of the

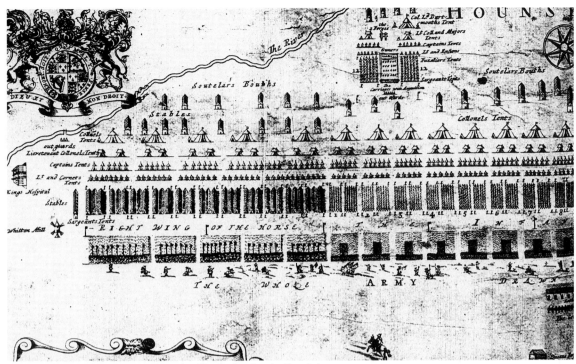

23. *Part of a map of the Camp on Hounslow Heath, showing the Hospital.*

24. *Sir Thomas Nott*

25. *Edward Montagu, Earl of Manchester; engraving by Dean after Lely*

26. *Edward Hyde, Earl of Clarendon; engraving by Thomason after Lely.*

Royal properties in Twickenham were sequestrated. They included houses bringing in rents of over £119 and two major houses, the manor house in Church Street and the house then on the site of Orleans House, which were together worth £1,500.

Otherwise, the impact of the Civil War was very much one of individuals and isolated incidents. A petition to the Commons in 1643 complained that the vicar of Twickenham, Dr Thomas Soame, indulged in 'superstitions and bowing to the altar' and had given thanks for the king's victory at Brentford. Those responsible for this petition included John Browne, Clerk to Parliaments, who lived at the manor house. In 1645 his orchards and fences were damaged by vandals 'who give out that they do it because he is a Roundhead.' Soame was imprisoned for a time, deprived of his living in 1646, but obtained another near Oxford, a royalist area.

When Charles I escaped from Hampton Court in November 1647 two of those involved had or were to have local connections. One was a Groom of the Bedchamber, William Murray, later Earl of Dysart, whose family lived in Ham House. The other was Sir John Berkeley, who had fought in the west with the Cornish army, and after the Restoration came to live at Twickenham Park as Lord Berkeley of Stratton. He lies, commemorated by a handsome memorial, in Twickenham church.

At the Restoration the Presbyterian minister, Thomas Willis, was deprived of the Twickenham living on the petition of a number of local individuals including John Browne, who had prudently changed sides. It was claimed that Willis had from the pulpit referred to Royalist plotters as 'malignants' and to the Stuarts as 'that Bloody Family'. But in due course, Willis conformed to the new regime and became a vicar of Kingston and even chaplain to Charles II.

Other personalities who played a part in the Civil War, and who at one time or another lived in Twickenham, included Edward, Earl of Manchester (a Parliamentary general), William Lenthall, Speaker of the House of Commons in the Long Parliament, Edward Hyde, Earl of Clarendon, Lord Belayse, mentioned above, and Lord Arundell, tenant of York House, who was either the Catholic Arundell of Wardour, of the Protestant Arundell of Trerice - both fought for the king in the west of England. Another was Sgt Birkhead, who lived in Twickenham in the 1650s. The Quaker, George Fox, visited Birkhead in 1658, shortly after seeing Cromwell at Hampton Court. Of the Lord Protector he said, 'I met him riding...at the head of his life-guard, I saw and felt a waft of death go forth against him, and when I came to him he looked like a dead man'. Cromwell died that September.

27. *Location of major houses in Twickenham on John Rocque's* Survey of the Country Round London *1741-45. This has been marked to show the houses there at the time of the map, and also of the sites of some built at a later date. The following is the key:*

1 Gordon House
2 Lacy House
3 St Margaret's
4 Twickenham Park
5 Cambridge Park
6 Marble Hill
7 Montpelier Row
8 Orleans House
9 Mount Lebanon and Riverside
10 Sion Row

11 York House and St Mary's Church
12 Poulett Lodge
13 Cross Deep
14 Pope's Villa
15 Radnor House
16 Strawberry Hill
17 Gifford Lodge
18 Heatham House
19 Kneller Hall
20 Whitton Park

Major Houses on the River Banks

The Thames has been a magnet for those who wished to build great houses in the parish. Downstream in medieval times there had been Twickenham Park, followed centuries later by Gordon House and the first - and second - St Margaret's House. Upstream of the ancient ferry to Richmond was Cambridge House, a mansion built by Sir Humphrey Lynde in about 1610-20; it was much enlarged by Sir Joseph Ashe in the 1650s, and earned its name during its occupation by Richard Owen Cambridge, friend of Dr Johnson and acquaintance of Horace Walpole, in the second half of the 18th century. The old house was finally demolished in the 1930s but its grounds had much earlier been nibbled away as what is now the Cambridge Park area was developed.

Next door still stands the palladian villa known as Marble Hill (so called after a piece of land anciently known as Marble Hill shot, but the reason for 'Marble' is still unknown). Built between 1724-28, it was the home of Henrietta Howard, one-time mistress of George II and the estranged wife of the Earl of Suffolk. She was also a close friend of Walpole and was acquainted with Dean Swift and John Gay. On her death in 1767, the house passed to her nephew, the Earl of Buckinghamshire. Subsequent occupants included Mrs Fitzherbert, the morganatic wife of the Prince of Wales, Lady Bath, the Duchess of Bolton, and the Marquess Wellesley. In 1825 the house passed into the possession of Jonathan Peel, a younger brother of the future prime minister, Sir Robert, and owner of a Derby winning horse in 1844. In 1887 it was bought by the Cunard family who planned to demolish the house and erect an estate of suburban houses on the grounds. They were bought out in 1902 by a consortium of local authorities and private donors, and the house and park were preserved for the general enjoyment of the public and the particular pleasure of Twickenham.

Beyond Marble Hill lies the Georgian row of houses

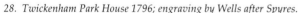

28. Twickenham Park House 1796; engraving by Wells after Spyres.

29. *Panoramic view of Twickenham's riverside. This oil painting on paper, apparently originally a pencil drawing, in private hands in Twickenham, shows various buildings, from Cross Deep on the left to St Mary's church on the right, which enable it to be dated between 1715 and 1734. A comparison with Peter Tillemans'* Prospect of the River Thames at Twickenham *of c1725 suggests that this panorama may have been a preliminary sketch for part of it.*

30. *Twickenham Meadows (later known as Cambridge House) 1803; engraving by Landseer after Webber.*

31. *Marble Hill House 1749; engraving by Mason after Heckell.*

32. Henrietta Howard, Countess of Suffolk, of Marble Hill; engraving by Greatbatch after Jervas.

known as Montpelier Row, built in the 1720s (but not for the 'maids of honour' of Mrs Howard, as is sometimes claimed!).

Next comes what remains of Orleans House. At one stage this estate also included all the land now occupied by Orleans Park School. A farm here was replaced by a substantial dwelling in 1663, and it was in this house that the then Princess Anne and her son the Duke of Gloucester stayed for one month in 1694. On the ayte (now part of the grounds) near the house, the young duke exercised his 'regiment' of boy soldiers. In due course the house passed to the Scottish politician, James Johnston (known as 'Secretary Johnston'), who demolished it and built a new one close by, designed by John James, who later went on to design the new church of St Mary's Twickenham in 1713. The famous Octagon was added to the house in about 1718, designed by another Scot, James Gibbs. George I was entertained here in July 1724, and George II's queen, Caroline of Ansbach, in 1729.

The house takes its name from the occupancy of Louis Philippe, duc d'Orleans, later King of the French, who was here 1815-17 - he revisited the house, in the company of Queen Victoria, in 1844.

A fashionable club was in residence in 1877 and the house finally became the home of the shipping mag-

33. Marble Hill Cottage 1831; engraving by Cooke after Barnard.

34. *Governor Pitt's House (later Orleans House) 1749; engraving by Mason after Heckell. Ragman's Castle is to the right.*

35. *York House c1808; engraving by J.P. Malcolm.*

36. The Earl of Radnor's House 1750; engraved by Walker after Heckell. Cross Deep House is to the right.

37. Radnor House as altered by H.E. Kendall for William Chillingworth c1850.

nate, William Cunard. It was after his death in 1906 that the estate was divided: the house and part of the grounds fell into the hands of a gravel company who demolished most of the house and extracted 200,000 tons of gravel. The rescue and restoration of the remains of the house are dealt with on p140.

Next door to Orleans House still stands the small 18th-century Riverside House, which had once belonged to the Countess of Suffolk and subsequently was acquired by the Duc d'Aumale, son of the Duc d'Orleans. Beyond that lay Lebanon House, owned in the first years of the 18th century by the Earl of Strafford, which was taken down in 1794. Its successor on the site, variously called Mount Lebanon or Lebanon House from the fine trees in the grounds, also had aristocratic occupants before it too was lived in by the Cunard family before they moved to Orleans House. By the turn of the century the grounds were being sold off for housing, and the house itself was used as a furniture store until it burnt down in December 1909.

Between what was Mount Lebanon and the church lay York House, the central portion of which is amongst the oldest surviving houses of this area. Built in about 1635 by Andrew Pitcarne, a Scot and a courtier, it was later the home of Edward Hyde, 1st Earl of Clarendon. It was fashionable again in 1790 when it was the home of the Austrian ambassador, Prince Strahemberg and in 1864 it was occupied by

38. Lawrence Hyde, Earl of Rochester, second son of Lord Clarendon, owned York House from 1676 until he sold it in 1689.

39. Sir John Hawkins, magistrate and author, of Twickenham House; engraving by R. Clamp after a painting by I. Roberts.

another of the Orleans princes, the Comte de Paris. The last owner was Sir Ratan Tata, a parsee merchant prince from Bombay, and after his death it was purchased as the home of Twickenham Borough Council.

Further upstream the Council already owned the old Richmond House, but this was demolished in the late 1920s, to be replaced in 1935 by municipal swimming baths (now abandoned). Nearby, Radnor House was also acquired by the Council. This old house, named after John Robartes, Earl of Radnor, was saved from demolition in the 1930s as a result of local pressure and support from Mrs Ionides and the late Queen Mary. Unfortunately, it was destroyed by bombing on 16 September 1940.

Many other substantial houses have now disappeared without trace including Poulett Lodge and most of the riverside houses along Cross Deep. Poulett Lodge, built after a fire had destroyed its predecessor in 1734, was named from Vere Poulett, later 3rd Earl Poulett; in the 1920s the Newborough Club occupied the premises, but they were taken down shortly after and the present Thames Eyot flats built.

Demolition also overtook the house occupied by Alexander Pope from 1719 until his death in 1744. A later owner, Lady Howe, had it taken down in 1808 and thereby earned herself the title of 'Queen of the Goths'. All that remains of Pope's villa is the grotto

40. Cross Deep Photograph by Alan Urwin.

41. *'Dr Batty's House' in 1780. Dr William Battie (1704-1776) was President of the Royal College of Physicians. He rebuilt the house in Cross Deep later known as Poulett Lodge in 1734.*

42. *Pope's Villa as altered by Sir William Stanhope c1788; aquatint by Guyot after Watts.*

lying beneath the buildings of the present day St Catherine's Convent school, the core of whose buildings is a house built by Thomas Young in 1842. The 'Queen of the Goths' built herself a new house a short distance upstream, half of which has survived bombing in the last war and is now known as Ryan House. The only old house to have survived on this stretch of the riverfront is that nowadays called Cross Deep. It was built in the 1690s, with later extensions in 1741 (by Gibbs) and 1780. In the 1780s it was occupied by George Shirley, one of the large family of the 1st Earl Ferrers (27 legitimate children by two marriages), and half brother to the 4th Earl who was hanged for murder in 1760.

The last major house that could be regarded as a riverside dwelling is Strawberry Hill. The name is derived from that of an old shot of land, forming part of the grounds. It is more fully described on pp 58-60.

Of the large inland houses, Kneller Hall is noted on pp 62, 87-90. Other buildings such as Twickenham House, the home of the magistrate and author, Sir John Hawkins, and Savile House, have been demolished. The 18th-century Amyand House, now forms part of the recently rebuilt St John's Hospital, and Heatham House is a Youth Centre.

Twickenham Notables

WRITERS

The brilliant philosopher and essayist, Francis Bacon (1561-1626), who came to grief politically through taking bribes, lived at Twickenham Park from about 1580 to 1608. He was followed as a resident by Lucy, Countess of Bedford (d1627); her circle of friends included John Donne and Ben Jonson. The connection of the poet, Sir John Suckling, with Whitton has already been described (see p19).

The 18th century was Twickenham's literary golden age. As we have seen in the previous chapter, the poet and satirist, Alexander Pope, lived in a villa on the river side of Cross Deep from 1719. Today, Pope's Grove, Grotto Road and Radnor Road indicate the boundaries of the garden that was once as well known as his poetry. His positioning of obelisks and other bounds to views, his preference for informality and use of the serpentine line, his regard for the 'genius' or particularity of a site, all made a contribution to landscape gardening in which we see his basically gentle and idealist nature at its purest. Pope was buried at St Mary's church, Twickenham, by the chancel steps. At first his only memorial was the tablet to his parents, but in 1761 Bishop Warburton erected a monument to Pope on the north wall of the gallery. On the north-east outside corner of the church wall is a plaque to his nurse, Mary Beach, to whom he may have owed his physical disability. Swift, the author of *Gulliver's Travels*, visited Pope here in 1726 and 1727, perhaps the key years of Twickenham as the country's literary centre. John Gay (1685-1732), creator of *The Beggar's Opera* was then enjoying the patronage of Kitty Hyde, Duchess of Queensberry, at Petersham. Contemporary with them was Lady Mary Wortley Montagu (1689-1762), a woman of beauty and intelligence, who in 1712 married Edward Wortley Montagu after an elopement. Most summers of the 1720s and 1730s she spent at Savile House, Heath Road - Saville Road now marks the site. (Her daughter, Lady Bute, to whom many of Lady Mary's letters are addressed, was to live in Montpelier Row from 1746 to 1748.) At first, Pope was quite bowled over by her precocity and looks, and commissioned a portrait of her by Kneller, which he retained in his best room for the rest of his days, but their friendship turned sour, perhaps because of her rejection of his regard. He attacked her scurrilously in verse and she responded with equal ferocity. Much of her later life was spent abroad as a some-

43. *Francis Bacon of Twickenham Park; engraving by S.Freeman*

44. *John Donne aged 18*

45. *Pope's Villa c1735; engraving by Parr after Rysbrack: the only picture of Pope's house published in his lifetime.*

46. *Pope's Grotto; engraving by Cary after Lewis.*

47. *Alexander Pope*

48. *Pope's Memorial to his parents and himself. Photograph by Robin Shotter.*

49. *Bishop Warburton's Memorial to Pope. Photograph by Robin Shotter*

what unfulfilled and isolated figure, but she continued to write her vivid, strong-minded letters to the end. Her second cousin, the novelist Henry Fielding (1707-54), lived in Back Lane, now Holly Road, from 1743 to 1748 and it is possible that he wrote part of *Tom Jones* there. She wrote: 'I am sorry for H Fielding's death, not only as I shall read no more of his writings, but I believe he lost more than others, as no man enjoyed life more than he did, though few had less reason to do so...'

Horace Walpole (1717-97), another outstanding letter-writer, moved to Strawberry Hill some three years after Pope's death - though he had met Pope at the age of eight. He proceeded to transform the dwelling into the Gothic extravaganza that we know today, though rooms were added in the 1860s by Lady Frances Waldegrave. Here Walpole wrote *The Castle of Otranto*, a pioneer of Gothic or horror novels; his book on Richard III, his histories and inventories, and his observant and expressive correspondence, all remain good reading today. He was a friend of Thomas Gray, whose odes he published at his Strawberry Hill press and it was Walpole's goldfish tub, in which the cat Selima drowned, which occasioned Gray's *Ode on the death of a favourite cat*.

Two minor poets were also in the vicinity. Richard Owen Cambridge (1717-1802) was at Cambridge Park, and Paul Whitehead (1710-74) at Colne Lodge on Twickenham Common. Fanny Burney (1752-1840), author of *Evelina* and *Diaries and Letters*, used to visit Cambridge and his son, George; she was assumed to have an 'understanding' with the latter but ended up marrying General d'Arblay, a French emigré.

50. Lady Mary Wortley Montagu

51. Horace Walpole as a young man.

Mary Wollstonecraft Godwin (1797-1851), author of *Frankenstein* and later the wife of Percy Bysshe Shelley, is said to have attended Miss Dutton's school at Fortescue House, London Road. Byron assisted her financially after Shelley's early death and in 1812 he visited Whitton Park, to which John Cam Hobhouse (1786-1869), statesman, author and Byron's executor, was heir.

Charles Dickens (1812-70) spent the summer of 1838 at 2 Ailsa Park Villas, St Margaret's, and the following summer in Petersham. *Oliver Twist* (1838) and *Nicholas Nickleby* (1839) will have been amongst the books engaging his thoughts at this time.

The 1850s saw H.G. Bohn, the publisher, at North End House, Richmond Road, and Alfred Tennyson (1809-92), Poet Laureate, was at Chapel House, Montpelier Row from March 1851 until November 1853. There he drank and smoked - he hid his pipe under a brick in the back wall of the house. He went for long walks and he wrote his *Ode on the death of the Duke of Wellington* (1852). His friend, F.T. Palgrave (1824-97), compiler of *The Golden Treasury*, was vice-principal at Kneller Hall from 1850 to 1855, when it was a training college for teachers of pauper and delinquent children - Frederick Temple, a future Archbishop of Canterbury, was principal at the time.

R.D. Blackmore (1825-1900), author of *Lorna Doone*, took a job in 1854 at the Wellesley House School, Hampton Road, and published two anonymous volumes of verse while he was there, before moving to Gomer House, Teddington, in 1857, from where he

pursued the vocations of market gardening and fiction.

In 1878 the song *Twickenham Ferry* was published by Theo Marzials (1850-1920), who retired from ill-health at the age of 32 yet still lived till his seventieth year. Flora Thompson, (1877-1947), author of *Lark Rise to Candelford*, was living at 8 Heathfield North at the time of her marriage to John Thompson at St Mary's church on 7 January 1903. In the summer of 1910 Virginia Stephen was in a nursing home at Burley, 15 Cambridge Park, again in February 1912, and for a few weeks in the summer of 1913. In 1912 she married Leonard Woolf, and in the following year she delivered the manuscript of *The Voyage Out*, her first novel, to Gerald Duckworth. In October 1914 she and Leonard spent a week at 65 St Margaret's Road before taking rooms at 17 The Green, Richmond; the parents of their 'Bloomsbury' familiar, Duncan Grant, lived at Grosvenor House, Grosvenor Road.

Walter de la Mare (1873-1956) came to live in South End House, Montpelier Row, overlooking Marble Hill Park, early in the last war. He occupied the house until his death. The novelist, Barbara Comyns, who died in the summer of 1992, spent her later years in a house with a pink pig in the window, which looked out on Twickenham Green. The house had once been a shop and features as such, indirectly, in *The House of Dolls*.

ARTISTS

The Thames in the vicinity of Twickenham has attracted artists since Tudor times. At first they were usually foreign visitors, mostly from the Low Countries and this continental element continued, reinforced by Huguenots and refugees from the French Revolution.

Although there was a great flowering of local artistic endeavour in the 18th century, it was the German jeweller, Augustin Heckel, who lived for many years in Richmond, that left us with the most detailed pictures of the Twickenham river front and the Flemish artist, Peter Tillemans, suffering from asthma and living on Richmond Hill, who painted views from there looking across the river, both in the 1730s.

Sir Godfrey Kneller's large house in Whitton, which he built in 1709, had a studio where he and a number of assistants worked - he left about 800 pictures to be sold at his death in 1723. Kneller was also churchwarden at St Mary's and was involved in the fundraising for a new church when the old one fell down in 1713.

Alexander Pope, who knew Kneller, studied painting under Charles Jervas, an Irishman who settled in Hampton. Jervas had at one time been Kneller's pupil and when Jervas was prosperous enough to own a coach and horses the old master slyly commented, "Ah! Mein Gott, if his horses draw no better than he does he will never get to his journey's end."

A portrait painter, Edward Seymour, lived in Twickenham from at least 1722 and was buried here in 1757. Thomas Hudson, who made a fortune from painting portraits, settled in a house in Cross Deep. William Hickey, then a boy, was a near neighbour, and he described Hudson's appearance in unflattering terms: 'His figure was rather grotesque being uncommonly low in stature, with a prodigious belly, and constantly wearing a large white bushy wig'. Hudson had been master of the young Joshua Reynolds, and when Sir Joshua was famous and moved to Wick House in Richmond, Hudson complacently remarked, "Little did I think we should ever have country seats opposite each other." Reynolds' retort was, "Little did I think when I was a young man that I should look down upon Mr Hudson."

Samuel Scott, the painter, was in Twickenham at the same time, living in a house opposite the parish church. He created many delightful river scenes, his pictures influenced, it is said, by Canaletto. Horace Walpole said of him, "the gout harassed and terminated his life". One of Scott's pupils was William Marlow, of whose paintings Walpole thought highly, but Marlow spent the last thirty years of his life in Twickenham in semi-retirement, amusing himself

53. Thomas Hudson, from a chalk drawing by Jonathan Richardson.

52. Sir Godfrey Kneller; self-portrait 1685.

54. *Anne Seymour Damer; engraving by Greatbatch after Cosway.*

55. *Francis Chantrey; engraving by Thomson after Raeburn.*

with making telescopes and similar objects in preference to painting. His landlord was John Curtis, a butcher, who himself took up painting under Marlow's tuition. In 1808 Joseph Farington, RA and gossip, cattily remarked of the seven Curtis children, "some of them were very like Marlow".

In the late 18th century John or James Spyers, a draughtsman, lived in Grosvenor House near the London Road. (Some of his prints of Twickenham Green appear in Bamber Gascoigne's *Images of Twickenham*.) In 1806 John Varley rented a house near Twickenham for the summer for himself and his pupils, John Linnell and William Henry Hunt. The duc de Montpensier, Louis Philippe's brother, was in Highshot House in Crown Road from 1800 to 1807; he was an early exponent of the new art of lithography. Nearby in Sion Row lived the Comte de Jarnac, a retired soldier and amateur artist (his watercolour sketch of Orleans House is part of the Ionides Collection).

When Louis Philippe returned to Twickenham in 1815, one of his ADCs, the general, Laurent Athalin, lived close by in Ferry House. Athalin's sketches of Twickenham riverside and Orleans House have survived as prints. Later still, in 1844, when King Louis Philippe visited England, his one-day visit to Twickenham was recorded by the French artist, Pringret.

Undoubtedly, J.M.W. Turner was the most famous artist who lived in Twickenham, and his time here is described on pp82-83. Thomas Rowlandson (1756-1827) does not appear to have lived in the locality but clearly visited on more than one occasion as a number of his drawings of the late 18th and early 19th century depict local scenes.

Amongst the artists living here at the turn of the century were talented amateurs such as Ethel Nesbitt and Laura Cunard of Orleans House. In more modern times Twickenham has been home to the late Eric Fraser, to Felix Gluck and to Lilian Dring.

As for sculptors, Michael Rysbrack may have been responsible for some of the figures in the Octagon at Orleans House; he definitely carved (and signed) the ornate memorial to Admiral Sir Chaloner Ogle in St Mary's church. Later there was the talented amateur, Mrs Damer, who lived first at Strawberry Hill and then at York House. Sir Francis Chantrey as a young man courted a maid who worked at Copt Hall, and went fishing with the butler there; he did

56. Robert William Edis; cartoon by Ape in Vanity Fair
11 *April 1885.*

57. Admiral Sir George Pocock

rather better financially in 1809 when he married his cousin, Mary Anne Wale, who brought with her a fortune of £10,000, in St Mary's church.

There are now many architects living in Twickenham, but the design of major buildings here has been mostly the work of non-residents. Among 18th-century figures are John James (Orleans House and the nave of St Mary's), James Gibbs (the Octagon Room of Orleans House and Whitton Park), Roger Morris (Marble Hill and Whitton Park), and Robert Adam (Gordon House). As a young man Sir Robert Edis, often known as 'Colonel' Edis from his involvement with the Artists' Rifles, designed the Mission Room, St John's Hospital and Newland House. In the 20th century Sir Albert Richardson was architect of the Chapel at St Mary's College, and gave advice on the re-ordering of the Sanctuary at St Mary's church.

NAVAL GENTLEMEN

The best known naval man in Twickenham was Admiral Sir George Pocock (1706-94). The outstanding event of his distinguished career was the capture of Havana in 1762: his share of the prize money was over £122,000. He settled in what became known as Orleans House in 1764, and is buried in the family grave in St Mary's church.

His grandson, Edward, also went into the navy, but was lost at sea in the Adriatic as a nineteen-year-old midshipman. He was serving there in 1813 under the command of that dashing frigate captain, William Hoste. Hoste retired due to ill health and lived for a time across the river at Ham and his widow later had a grace-and-favour residence at Hampton Court. Hoste's daughter, Priscilla, became the mistress of the Earl of Kilmorey, one-time resident of Orleans House; she lies buried with the Earl in the mausoleum opposite the Ailsa Tavern in St Margaret's.

Naval tradition in Twickenham began even earlier. Lord Berkeley, who lived in Twickenham Park

58. Admiral Sir Chaloner Ogle.

Park until 1830, and Captain Foy of the East India sailing fleet was at Highshot House, Crown Road from 1819-25. Rear-Admiral James Burney, Fanny's brother, lived in Twickenham, and in 1861, when he was aged 67, was at 9 Copt Hall Villas in Clifden Road.

In the present times there has been a local historian who fought in the Mediterranean and then had a hand in the planning of Mulberry Harbour; to say nothing of Captain Shaw RN of Orleans Road, who served as a midshipman on a battleship at Jutland in World War I, and at the end of World War II commanded the battleship, HMS *King George V*.

A FIRST EDITION IN MARBLE

St Mary's church possesses the first edition of a poem - even if not a very distinguished one - by John Dryden as an epitaph to Frances, fourth daughter of Sir William Brooke. She was one of the beauties of the court of Charles II and was painted by Sir Peter Lely in portraits which are now in Hampton Court; when she died in 1690, her second husband, Mathew Harvie, had a marble monument erected in the pew in which he and his wife sat, and to judge from the surviving marks on the church floor, this was in the centre aisle. Dryden's engraved poem reads as follows:

Faire kind and true! A Treasure each alone:
A Wife a Miftrefs and a Freind in one.
Reft in this Tomb, rais'd at thy Husbands cost,
Here, fadly summing what he had, & lost.

59. Frances Brooke, later Lady Whitmore, from the painting by Lely at Hampton Court.

in the latter half of the 17th century, had two naval sons: Charles was a captain and died at sea of small-pox in 1682, and his brother John was an admiral at the age of 26, and died before he was 35 years old in 1697. A kinsman of the Berkeley family (hence his burial in the family vault in St Mary's) was Admiral Byron ('Foulweather Jack'), who died in 1786: he was the grandfather of the poet.

Sir Chaloner Ogle's major exploit was his defeat, when in command of the *Swallow*, of the pirate Bartholomew Roberts off West Africa in 1722. A somewhat peppery individual, he quarrelled with Edward Trelawney, Governor of Jamaica, in 1742, but this does not seem to have hindered his promotion as he became Commander-in-Chief of the Navy in 1749. His home in Twickenham was the house later known as Gifford Lodge, facing the Common, and he became a Trustee of St Mary's School.

In the 1850s Vice-Admiral Lysaght lived in Heath Lane Lodge. Other notable naval men included Admiral Fox at Copt Hall sometime in the 18th century, and Commander Woollnough who lived close to the Swan on the riverside in the 1830s - his son, Joseph, was later curate at St Mary's. The sailor prince, the Duke of Clarence (later William IV), was at Bushy

60. *The Whitmore-Harvie memorial in St Mary's church; Dryden's poem is on the right side. Photograph by Robin Shotter.*

Come, Virgins, er'e in equall bands you joine
Come firft, and Offer at Her facred fhryne;
Pray for but halfe the Virtues of this Wife
Compound for all the reft wth longer life
And wish your Vowes like her's may be return'd
So lov'd when living and when dead so mourn'd.

This can presumably be regarded as the first edition, as it was probably inscribed on the memorial soon after her death, but did not appear in print until *Examen Poeticum* in 1693.

Harvie himself died in 1694, leaving £100 to the parish on condition that the memorial continued to remain in situ, but it was in fact moved several times; the first was probably when the church was rebuilt in 1714. The substantial marble memorial now stands behind the choir stalls on the south side of the church.

61. *Thomas Wentworth, Earl of Strafford.*

'YOUR MOST INFENIT AFFECTIONAT MOTHER'

Among Twickenham's letter-writers there can have been none as entertaining and unselfconscious (not to mention as eccentric in spelling) as Lady Wentworth. As Isabella Apsley, she was born about 1653; her father, Sir Allen Apsley, was Treasurer of the Household of the Duke of York, later James II, and she herself became a Lady of the Bedchamber to Mary of Modena, James' queen. Her husband, Sir William Wentworth, died in 1692, and her strong maternal instincts were then concentrated on her son, Thomas, who was created Earl of Strafford in 1711 and who was from 1701 a resident of a house by the river at Twickenham. Owing to his duties in Prussia he spent little time in Twickenham, but his mother, who loved 'sweet Twitnum', often spent the summer there.

It was from this house that she penned many of her letters to her son, constantly expressing her love for her 'dearest and best of children' (though contemporary opinion was rather less flattering of him), endeavouring to find him suitable brides. Her other matchmaking preoccupation was with her somewhat uncouth daughter, Betty, who lived with her. Next to her family she loved her pets, or 'dums', particularly her monkey Pug, and her dog Fubs, on

62. Lord Strafford's house at Twickenham 1711.

whose death in 1708 she wrote a very moving letter. Perhaps in answer to a criticism of this devotion, she wrote 'I hate cards and Tables and old peopple must have som devertion.'

Another love was gossip, and her letters record many a local scandal. Lady Mary Tudor, the illegitimate daughter of Charles II, was married to the 2nd Earl of Derwentwater in 1687, and within a month of his death in 1705 had remarried a Mr Graham, only to be widowed again two years later. She was not to be a widow for long. Isabella recorded that 'last Tewsday came and went in her moarning coach for Mr Grims to church, and was marryed to Jamse Roock, Coll. Roock's son. Grims had been dead not thre qrs. of a year yet; she turned Lady Tuften's children out of the church and said she would not be marryed tel they went out. She was marryed in whit sattin. She has setled fower hundred a year upon him for her life, and the rest she keeps for her self and hous. She ows a great deal of money hear; he sent the ringers twoe ginneys and his mother sent half a one, and his mother is as fonde of her as I should be of your bryde...'

A notorious local character was the gambler (and possibly bigamist) Thomas Boucher of Heath Lane Lodge, who died in 1708. Of him, Lady Wentworth wrote, '...thear was a paper put upon the church door in virs about his many wivs, they say he has fower. Its not known yett what he has left; twoe old wemen was over hard to be very wety seying, why had he noe scutchyons, for he might have good arms, a pack of cards, a dyse box, and quarter a pair of sissors.'

Isabella was delighted by Thomas' marriage to Anne Johnson in 1711 and the birth of a daughter, Anne; in the summer of 1714 at Twickenham - 'I carryed her to the common and she was highly delighted to see the Rabits run about.' It was not until 1722 that Betty, now aged 41, found a husband. By then Thomas had retired from public life and spent much time in Yorkshire; Isabella passed her latter years in Twickenham and her last surviving letter, May 1733, written for her, ends in her own shaky hand 'yr most afft. Mother IW'. She died in August.

The riverside house, which had been neglected, was pulled down in 1794 on the instructions of her daughter-in-law Anne, who had married the Hon. William Connolly; in its place a house later known as Mount Lebanon was built, but this was demolished after a fire in 1909, and several smaller houses now occupy the site.

'SWEET LASS OF RICHMOND HILL?'

Among local residents about whom legends cluster is Mary Anne (always known as Maria) Fitzherbert. The daughter of Walter Smythe of Acton Burnell, a staunch Roman Catholic, she was twice widowed after marriages to older men when, at the age of 27, she came to London under the aegis of her uncle, Lord Sefton, in 1784. She soon attracted the attention of the pleasure-loving George, Prince of Wales, who was only 21.

She is believed to have been living in Richmond at this time (though the house has not been identified), and this fact, together with the line 'I would crowns resign to call her mine' has led to the suggestion that the popular song of the period, *Sweet Lass of Richmond Hill*, refers to her. It seems certain that the song originally referred to Frances I'Anson of Richmond in Yorkshire, but in London society it may well have been taken to refer to the Prince of Wales's devotion to Mrs Fitzherbert.

Though undoubtedly attracted to him, she would not consent to become his mistress, and marriage to a Roman Catholic would have excluded him from the succession. But George pressed her to marry him by fair means and foul, and in December 1785 she consented. They were married in the drawing room of Mrs Fitzherbert's London house on 15 December by the Rev. Robert Burt. Burt has been much traduced in historical works as a seedy adventurer, released from a debtor's prison for the occasion, but he was a member of a wealthy family with extensive interests in the West Indies, and had been a chaplain to the Prince for at least eighteen months. In 1788 he became vicar of Twickenham, but after three years of conscientious work there died of a fever at the age of 34. A certificate signed by bride and bridegroom is now in the Royal Archives; the marriage was certainly illegal, since it did not have the king's permission, but it appears to be canonically valid to both the Roman Catholic and Anglican churches.

After nearly ten years, George abruptly broke off their relationship. Debt-ridden, he had decided to make a 'suitable' marriage for dynastic reasons, and in April 1795 was married to the uncouth and indiscreet Princess Caroline of Brunswick. By this time Mrs Fitzherbert had moved to Marble Hill, Twickenham, and on the eve of the royal wedding was surprised to see the Prince ride past her house. She remained there only a few months - though a visit to Strawberry Hill is on record - and moved to Ealing in October.

The Prince's marriage was a disaster, and in 1796 he wrote a long will, proclaiming his devotion to 'my Maria Fitzherbert, my wife, the wife of my heart & soul'. He urged her to return to him, and after three years, during which she received assurance from Rome that her marriage was valid, she did so. By now

63. *Miniature of Miss Smythe, later Mrs Fitzherbert.*

a stout middle-aged couple, they spent much time at Brighton, but the fickle Prince came under the influence of Lady Hertford and in 1811 he and Maria finally separated. She thus had no share in the Regency or in his reign as George IV, but as he lay dying in 1830 she sent him a letter of affectionate regard: it is not known if he ever read it, but in accordance with his wishes of many years before, he was buried with Maria's miniature portrait round his neck. She was treated with great kindness and esteem by William IV and Queen Adelaide, and died at the age of 80 in 1837, three months before the accession of Victoria. Her memorial statue in St John the Baptist church, Brighton, has three wedding rings.

64. *River traffic, including rowing boat, horses on the Surrey bank towing a barge, and sailing vessel in engraving of 1749.*

Twickenham's River

RIVER TRAFFIC

Over the centuries the relative levels of the land and the river hereabouts have varied. At the time of the Romans the tide reached only as far upstream as London Bridge. Opposite Syon Park, a mile downstream of the Twickenham parish boundary, a rectangular hut of about 35 feet long of *c*AD200 to 300 was built on piles driven into the river bed at a point just below the present low water level at the time of spring tides. The floor of this hut, made of layers of wattle and green clay, was only 19 inches above the natural gravel, showing that the river wasn't tidal

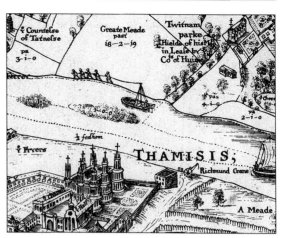

65. *Detail from Moses Glover's map of 1635 showing men on the Middlesex bank towing a barge.*

the river as far as Staines. When commercial barge traffic began after the Norman period is not recorded but there must always have been some boats working the river. In time the traffic below Staines came to be regulated by the Court of Common Council of the City of London. Moses Glover's map of the manor of Syon shows a team of five men towing a barge on the Twickenham bank; the towpath ran from the ferry at Gordon House, where the river Crane joins the Thames. Downstream of this the towpath was on the Surrey bank on which horses were permitted to tow boats.

In 1777 tolls for the use of the towpath amounted to ½d per ton from London to Brentford, 1d to Richmond, 1½d to Teddington, 2d to Kingston etc., but private boats of less than three tons were exempt until 1870. In 1789 the towpath was moved from Twickenham to the Richmond bank, causing great troubles with riparian householders in Richmond, who were only appeased by the towpath being built in the river below their gardens.

As population increased in the 19th century hygiene was also a problem for the whole of the Twickenham riverside as all sewage went into the river. This was only solved at the end of the century when the Half Tide Barrier was built to maintain the river level.

Trouble with the river level and the depth of water continued late into the 19th century. When the old London Bridge, which slowed down the flow of water, was taken down the flow of water increased. The average level at Richmond Bridge in the 1820s fell by about three or four feet as a result. Also after 1855 water began to be extracted at Hampton for domestic use and navigation, as a consequence, was often impossible.

and also not subject to any great change in water level. By 1770, when the great canal builder James Brindley surveyed this part of the Thames, he said that vessels of 100 tons could reach Isleworth, but only with the help of tides, and Thomas Bowen, in his map of 1777, recorded that the river was tidal only as far as Richmond and Twickenham.

Now the rise and fall of the river at Richmond bridge due to tides, measures 5½ metres at spring tides and 3 metres at neaps.

The *Anglo-Saxon Chronicle* records that the then shallow draft Saxon and Viking boats did come up

66. *Twickenham Ferry from a postcard c1908. Ferry Cottage is on the left.*

TWICKENHAM FERRY AND RICHMOND BRIDGE

For centuries the only bridges across the lower reaches of the Thames were London Bridge and Kingston Bridge, and the main means of crossing the river was by ferry. The earliest ferry in the Twickenham locality was Richmond Ferry, dating from the 15th century or earlier, near the site of Richmond Bridge, but the most famous is Twickenham Ferry. Legend gives it an origin in the reign of King John, but the most likely date of its inception is about 1640. It was set up by William Murray, later 1st Earl of Dysart and the owner of Ham House, to provide a link between the grounds of his house and the nearest accessible point on the Twickenham side (Eel Pie Island prevented a direct route to Twickenham village). It was leased for years to local watermen, and occasionally women, though from time to time there were attempts by others to run a rival service.

The foundation stone of Richmond Bridge was laid in 1774, and following its opening in 1777 Richmond Ferry ceased to operate; this development, however, had little effect on Twickenham Ferry, whose traffic was with Ham and Petersham.

In 1878 *Twickenham Ferry*, a 'river ditty' by Theo Marzials was published, and became a popular bal-lad, with its evocation of a romantic river crossing.

'O hoi, and O ho', you may call as you will,
The moon is a-rising on Petersham Hill,
And with love like a rose in the stern of the wherry,
There's danger in crossing to Twickenham Town.

The Ferry was to become famous for another reason some thirty years later. Following the opening of Marble Hill Park to the public and the designation of the towing path on the Surrey side as a public highway, Walter Hammerton, a member of a long-established family of watermen, set up a boathouse near Marble Hill and also began ferrying passengers across the river. After some desultory legal exchanges, Lord Dysart and the Twickenham ferryman, William Champion, brought an action against Hammerton, claiming sole ferry rights between Ham and Twickenham. The case, heard in April 1913, decided in Hammerton's favour on the grounds that he was dealing with new traffic. The Earl appealed and the judgement was reversed, but Hammerton, a determined man, appealed in the Lords and the decision was again reversed, this time in his favour. This victory was marked by the publication of a song by Arthur M. Young and W.F. Clarke called *Hammerton's*

67. *The New Bridge at Richmond; engraving of 1780*

Ferry: The Ferry to Fairyland, which is interesting for the occasion and its elaborate title page, but as a song lacks the charm of Marzial's ballad.

About 1870 Jesse Barrow, an emigrant to Australia, set up Twickenham Ferry across the Yarra River on the outskirts of Melbourne; it was run by the family until 1934, when the Grange Road Bridge was constructed and the ferry closed.

Twickenham Ferry no longer runs, and is a sad sight, with weed-covered slipway and rotting ferry-boat; Ferry Cottage, built for the ferryman by Dysart early in the century, is no longer connected with it.

68. *Twickenham Ferry in Australia*

Twickenham at Prayer

WHEN THE PARISH CHURCH FELL DOWN

The date of origin of the parish of Twickenham is unknown; the first dated vicar is William Browne, in 1332, but he certainly had predecessors. The tower of the present church, dedicated, like so many in Thameside villages, to St Mary the Virgin, is of Kentish ragstone and dates from about the 14th century; there was a nave of the same material but from about 1700 the church records indicate that the building was in a bad state of repair - the vestry meeting of 10 January 1704 requested that the church-wardens 'doe take speedy care' to carry out repairs, and there are many similar entries. By 1713 the situation was serious, and Dr Samuel Prat, the newly appointed vicar was so alarmed that, according to Lady Wentworth, he 'preached one sarment in it, but would preach noe more, but ordred Passmore to make a tabernakle in the church yard, which al has and must contrebute to.' A meeting in the church to discuss repairing or rebuilding it was arranged for 18 April, but the issue had been settled by then; Vestry minutes of 25 April laconically record 'The parish church of Twickenham falling down on Thursday night the 9th Aprill 1713, The Rebuilding of the Church Taken into consideration.' The newly-appointed churchwarden, court painter Sir Godfrey Kneller, took the lead in establishing a subscription list (still preserved in the church archives) and engaging an architect. This was John James of Greenwich (1672-1746) who had already worked locally in the garden of James Johnston's house. The nave, built in red brick in contemporary style, was larger than that which had fallen, and as the marks of the roof against the tower still indicate, taller than its predecessor.

The work was carried out by a group of local craftsmen - builders, bricklayers, blacksmiths, glaziers etc - only the woodcarver came from as far as Richmond. There is a gap in the parish accounts for this period, but it is known that the committee deal-

70. Richard Meggot, Vicar of Twickenham 1668-1692.

69. Modern photograph of St Mary's church showing the medieval tower and red-brick nave by John James

71. *St Mary's church; engraving by Parkyns after Barrow, 1790. Riverside warehouses are seen on the left, the old Vicarage stands in front of the Church, and Dial House, now the Vicarage, is on the right.*

ing with the rebuilding failed to meet the bills, and was taken to court by the unpaid craftsmen. As a result, the committee, despite trying to evade responsibility, was ordered to settle the accounts. It turned on those who had failed to honour their promises of donations or pay the relevant rates, and in 1717 it was decided to draw the names of defaulters out of a hat and proceed against them in the order thus settled. Ten years later there was still some money outstanding and a house to house collection was organised to clear it.

THE GROWTH OF LOCAL PARISHES
The rebuilt church continued with very little alteration for nearly 150 years, but the growth of population and the lack of space in St Mary's led to the creation of a new parish of Holy Trinity (1841) with a church facing Twickenham Green. The Rev. G.S. Master, vicar of St Mary's 1859-65, not only altered the interior of his church to make more seating, but initiated the creation of a Whitton parish, with its church of St Philip and St James (1862). The growing size of East Twickenham resulted in the formation of a new parish of St Stephen, which continued the evangelical tradition of the Montpelier Chapel it had replaced. The last division of the old parish of

Twickenham came when the mission district of St Martin became the parish of All Hallows (1939) with a Wren tower, brought stone by stone from London, beside its red brick nave. Further subdivisions of Holy Trinity and St Philip and St James parishes resulted in the new parishes of All Saints (1914) and St Augustine (1958) respectively.

72. *Holy Trinity church, Twickenham Green, as originally built in 1841; engraving from the* Illustrated London News, *22 Aug 1846.*

73. *St Stephen's church before the tower was built in 1907.*

NONCONFORMISTS

Twickenham's first place of worship for non-Anglicans was opened in 1800 for the Methodists. It was in Holly Road and the building still stands, although now occupied by John Davidson, shopfitters. There was considerable opposition to it from some quarters: it was reported that 'as the Winter drew on, and the Evening Service was held by Candlelight, Satan stirred up the Rabble from the Public House to disturb the congregation; and as they could not be discovered in the Dark, they triumphed in their shameless Practices. No woman could attend in the Evening with any Kind of Comfort. In Addition to the Indecencies the Rabble proceeded to throw Stones among the congregation.' A new chapel was opened in 1881 in Queen's Road; this in its turn was replaced by a larger building seating some 600 people in 1889.

The next chapel to be built was opened in 1844 by the Independents (later Congregationalists, now United Reformed Church) in First Cross Road. They had previously worshipped in a building known as Lady Shaw's School Room, which lay to the north of the present church, and is now the church hall. The chapel was rebuilt in its present form in 1866.

The first Baptist chapel on Twickenham Green was opened in 1853 and is shown in the photograph reproduced here. It was replaced by the present building in 1915.

The London City Mission worked amongst the poor of Twickenham and Whitton during the second half of the last century. One of the first missionaries to work in Twickenham stated that he had witnessed more ungodliness and sin in the town than when he had been labouring in the West Indies. 'It is painful to witness the entire disregard to spiritual things, which prevails through the whole district...It is lamentable that the majority of people devote the sacred hours of the Sabbath to matters connected with their temporal concerns. The men cultivate their gardens &c., in the forenoon, and read the newspapers, or something akin to them, during the remainder of the day. The women wash, iron, and go to work, as on other days. These, and in many cases, far more deadening engagements, find the people lulling their consciences into total forgetfulness of all that is high, holy and good.'

The Salvation Army hall on Twickenham Green, now no. 26, was opened in 1893. It was replaced in 1924 by a new hall in May Road; the present hall was opened in 1958.

In St Margaret's, Avenue Baptist church was opened in 1880 at the junction of St Margaret's Road, Winchester Road and The Avenue. A new church was built in 1905, but as it stood in the path of the Chertsey Road, constructed in the 1930s, it had to be demolished in 1932. The compensation received went towards the building of the Baptist church at Whitton.

Nonconformists in Whitton first met in a private house. The Whitton Gospel Mission was founded in

74. (Left) The Methodist chapel in Holly Road, opened in 1800; the first chapel built in Twickenham.

75. (Above) Twickenham Congregational Chapel (now United Reformed Church) built in 1844.

76. The second and third Methodist churches in Twickenham opened in 1881 and 1899 respectively; the 1899 buiding on the right was demolished in 1986.

77. *The London City Mission c1898.*

78. Twickenham Baptist chapel on the Green, opened in 1853 and replaced by the present building in 1915.

1881; they opened a gospel hall in Nelson Road (now occupied by Hollygrove Flooring Co. Ltd). It was run by local committees on Brethren lines until it was replaced by the new Baptist chapel in Hounslow Road in 1935.

Other nonconformist churches to be found in the borough include the independent Baptist chapel in Amyand Park Road (now Amyand Park Independent Evangelical Church) founded in 1888; the Free Grace Baptist chapel in Powder Mill Lane, now meeting in former Salvation Army premises; and Whitton Methodist church in Percy Road, an off-shoot of the Twickenham branch, was formed in the 1930s.

Joanna Southcott (1750-1814) is said to have lived for time in a cottage close to the junction of Campbell Road and the Staines Road. She was known as the 'Prophetess of Exeter' for her claim that she was to be the mother of a second Messiah. By 1810 there was a chapel of her followers in Teddington, whose membership included fourteen adherents from Twickenham.

79. Joanna Southcott

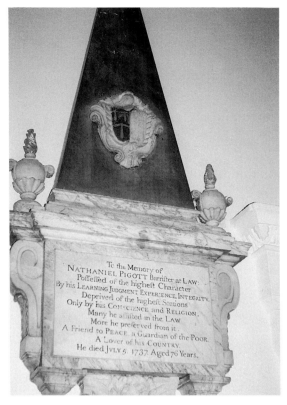

*80. Nathaniel Pigott's memorial in St Mary's church.
Photograph by Robin Shotter.*

81. Interior of St James' Roman Catholic church, pre 1960.

ROMAN CATHOLICS

Various records indicate the presence of Roman Catholics in Twickenham, and particularly in Whitton, from the 17th century. Alexander Pope was a Catholic, as was his friend the distinguished lawyer, Nathaniel Pigott, but both were buried in St Mary's church. Pope wrote the inscription on Pigott's memorial, which not only includes the typical quip 'Many he affifted in the Law: More he preferred from it', but also comments, 'Deprived of the higheft Stations Only by his Conscience and Religion'. The nearest Roman Catholic place of worship appears to have been in Isleworth, and Walpole writes of his niece observing from the window of Lacy House Catholics crossing the ferry from Richmond to Isleworth on Sundays at the expense of Lord Shrewsbury; she 'has counted an hundred in one day at a penny each...'

A church was opened in Grosvenor Road in 1883, replaced two years later by the church of St James in Pope's Grove. A mission was established in St Margaret's in 1930, and the temporary church of St Margaret of Scotland in St Margaret's Road opened eight years later. This was replaced by a permanent building in 1969. St Edmund's church, Whitton, originated in a mission commenced in 1934.

In 1927 St Mary's Training College for Roman Catholic teachers, under the Vincentian Order, was opened in Strawberry Hill, which had been purchased for the purpose four years earlier by the Catholic Education Council. Its original buildings have been meticulously preserved and others added. In post-war years the buildings have been further extended, women students admitted, and the curriculum broadened to the general degree course of Surrey University, of which it is now a college, though the Vincentian link will continue.

St Catherine's School, in buildings on the site of Pope's Villa, was founded by the Sisters of Mercy in 1914 and took its name from its first home, in Vicarage Road. In 1916 it moved to Orford Lodge, Pope's Grove, and in 1919 to its present location. In 1992 the Sisters, following a change of policy, transferred the School to an independent Roman Catholic trust.

Seats for the Gentry

MONTPELIER AND SION ROWS

Montpelier and Sion Rows were developed early in the 1720s by Captain John Gray, although there is some debate as to which of the two was the first to be built. Gray appears to have acquired the land and then sub-contracted to builders or other developers. Originally Montpelier Row consisted of seventeen (now fifteen) houses, Montpelier Chapel (demolished in the 1940s), and then a gap and a further five houses ending with South End House. Why the Row was called Montpelier is not known, although it resembled that famous health resort of France, Montpellier, where the great Earl of Clarendon spent some of his last years in exile.

The names given to most of the houses in the Row are of 19th and 20th century origin. Residents tended to become more aristocratic as the 18th century pro-gressed, and included Lady Bute, the Countess of Buchan, the Earl of Macclesfield, Lord Hillsborough, as well as a successful tailor and an oriental scholar.

Samuel Tolfrey, who lived at No. 4 from 1811, had been a lawyer and a government servant in India and Ceylon; during his retirement he supervised the education in England of two young Singalese, J.H. de Saram (who was eventually ordained) and Balthazar de Saram. Tolfrey moved from Twickenham about 1817 to find a more suitable climate for his gout.

Sion Row was built almost certainly in 1721 in a similar mellow brick, but on a smaller scale. As late as the 1760s John Gray's only son, Tufton, still owned half the houses in Sion Row. Most the inhabitants tended to be steady but prosperous local people, unlikely to rival the inhabitants of Montpelier Row. They included the author, Laetitia Hawkins and her scholarly brother 'Harry Classic', a French royalist exile, the Comte de Jarnac, and the first local historian of Twickenham, Edward Ironside. He was the son of a Lord Mayor of London and earned his living as an East India Company supercargo.

82. Montpelier Row, 1900; lithograph by Thomas Way.

83. Sion Row 1900; lithograph by Thomas Way

THE MANOR HOUSE

The origin of the manor of Twickenham and its subdivisions of land remain a mystery. In 1086 Twickenham was part of the manor of Isleworth, but later the manorial lands seem to have been divided into three parts, one of which was centred on the manor house which lay between Church and York Streets. Later, possibly only in the 19th century, the house became known as Arragon House because of a tradition (for which there is no evidence) that Henry VIII's queen was connected with the manor. In 1800 the land surrounding the house was extensive, stretching back from Church Street to Amyand Park Road (York Street was not formed until 1899) and in the other direction from Oak Lane to London Road. The house itself seems to have been of the Tudor period - in the 1660s it had sixteen hearths.

The estate was given to Henrietta Maria on her marriage to Charles I in 1625, sold during the Commonwealth period, restored to her subsequently and, on her death, it passed to Catherine of Braganza, Charles II's queen. The most notable residents of the house were John Browne (c1608-1691), Clerk of the Parliaments, from 1638 until his death, and the painter, Samuel Scott, in the mid-18th century.

Most of the house was demolished in the 1850s and the remnant, known as Arragon Tower, was taken down in 1934, when the Tudor bricks were removed for use at Hampton Court.

84. 'Arragon Tower', the last remaining portion of the Manor House demolished in 1934.

85. Map of 1805 in the Land Revenue Record Office showing the Manor House and Park.

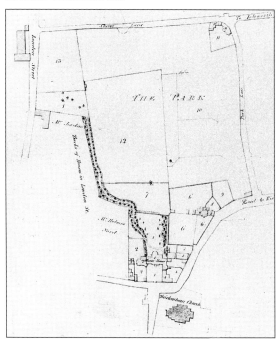

TWICKENHAM GREEN

Beyond the parish lockup and stocks and the pump lay the Little Common of Twickenham. By the 18th century smart villas were being built on both sides of it on what are now the Hampton and Staines Roads, and its appearance in mid-century can be seen in Boydell's engraving below. Twickenham House, on the extreme left of the picture, was the home from 1760 to 1771 of Sir John Hawkins (see p29), magistrate, writer, and friend and biographer of Samuel Johnson. He was, however, given to litigation, and sued a neighbour for damage to his wall by nailing fruit trees to it. He received one shilling damages.

The house in the centre was occupied by Admiral Sir Chaloner Ogle, and after his death in 1750 by Lord Kingston, who married his widow. After him the house was owned by Frances, widow of the 4th Marquess of Tweeddale, and acquired its name of Gifford Lodge, since the Earldom of Gifford was a subordinate title of the Marquess. Laetitia Hawkins recalled her 'whooping voice', and her eccentricities, including a dominating attitude to family and acquaintance. She commented of the Marchioness:

"She had been left, I suppose, early in life a widow. I have indeed heard it said, that she 'worried,' as it is called, her gouty lord out of his life, by her tender solicitudes; - but I am sure if she did so, it was with a perfectly good intention, for his memory still remained very dear to her."

The Little Common's name was changed to

86. A View taken on Twickenham Common; drawn and engraved by T. Boydell, 1753. Visible on the left is Twickenham House; in the centre, Lord Kingston's house, formerly owned by Admiral Sir Chaloner Ogle and later known as Gifford Lodge. To the right is the house of Abraham Prado. The coach is making for Hampton.

Twickenham Green after the Enclosure of 1818; at this time the land was set aside as compensation to the poor of the parish for the loss of fuel and other rights on the former common lands. In 1820 the Vicar and Churchwardens leased the Green for twenty-one years, on condition that it be 'open for the free and uninterrupted ingress and egress of all persons for the purpose of walking and recreation public games and sports and all amusements (the Game of Quoits Bull baiting Badger baiting or any other games that have a riotous or immoral tendency excepted) and for the erecting of Booths for Cricket matches without demanding or requiring any compensation'. Two 'accustomed fairs' were to be allowed, but otherwise 'there be not permitted or suffered any Moun-

tebanks Shows or Plays to be exhibited or performed... The land continued to be leased to private individuals until 1868, when it was leased out to the new Twickenham Local Board of Health for £35 per annum. In the same year the annual fair, which had caused considerable damage to the land, was discontinued.

Meanwhile there was a considerable growth of population on both sides of the Green, and this was the reason for the creation of the new Parish of Holy Trinity in 1841. The Green is still a popular centre for recreation, sports, and open air services and meetings of all sorts.

STRAWBERRY HILL

When Horace Walpole bought his 'Gothic Toy' in 1747 it was merely a cottage, 'a little new farm out of Twickenham' recently inhabited by the dramatist Colley Cibber. He soon began to build his gables, cloisters, battlements, towers and turrets, using the architecture of all ages and much lath and plaster. He referred to it as his 'Gothic Castle' and 'Gothic Abbey', and to himself as the 'Abbot of Teddington'.

The inside was the equal of the outside with ornaments, books, pictures and curios from everywhere, and 'every piece of furniture a curiosity'. His correspondence and literary output were prodigious, much of it showing his affection for the district, notably commemorated in his *Parish Register of Twickenham*. The poem which he wrote jointly with Lord Bath stood up for Strawberry Hill:

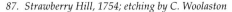

Some cry up Gunnersbury
For Sion some declare
And some say that with Chiswick House
No villa can compare;
But ask the beaux of Middlesex
Who know the country well,
If Strawberry Hill, if Strawberry Hill
Don't bear away the bell?

Walpole recounts an incident when he was on his way to dine with the Duke and Duchess of Montrose at Twickenham Park. 'Lady Browne and I were going to the Duchess of Montrose at seven o'clock. The evening was very dark. In Twickenham lane under her park-pale a black figure on horseback pushed by between the chaise and the hedge on my side. I suspected it was a highwayman, when I heard a voice cry 'Stop!' and the figure came back to the chaise. He said, 'Your purses and your watches!' I replied, 'I have no watch.' 'Then your purse!' I gave it to him; it had nine guineas. Lady Browne also gave him her purse, and was going to hand her watch, but he said, 'I am much obliged to you, I wish you goodnight', pulled off his hat, and rode away. 'Well,' said I, 'Lady Browne, you will not be afraid of being robbed another time, for you see there is nothing in it.' 'Oh, but I am', said she; and now I am in terror lest he should return, for I have given him a purse with only bad money that I carry on purpose.'

The Waldegrave family were later owners of the house. The widow of the 7th Earl, Fanny, was a great political hostess here in the 1860s and 1870s.

In 1927 Strawberry Hill became a Roman Catholic Teachers' Training College and is now an integral part of the University of Surrey.

87. Strawberry Hill, 1754; etching by C. Woolaston

88. Strawberry Hill, by Thomas Rowlandson.

89. The Library, Strawberry Hill; engraving by Jackson after Tiffin.

90. *View of the chapel in the garden at Strawberry Hill, 1784; engraving by Godfrey after Pars.*

Most ice houses were excavated below ground level, lined with brick, with a drain at the bottom to remove water; above ground the well was covered with the earth removed and occasionally more insulation was added. The entrance was usually by a short tunnel underneath the mound at ground level, with double doors and other more sophisticated designs to exclude summer heat. The shapes varied: there was much argument as to whether they should be planted with trees or at least shaded with them, as at Marble Hill, and architects also competed by designing elegant, tasteful and conspicuous above ground structures.

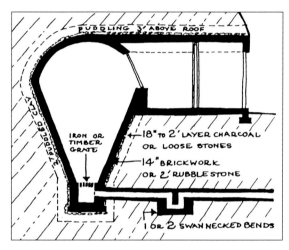

91. *Design of an ice house.*

LOCAL ICE HOUSES

The only Ice House still in being in Twickenham is in the Plantation alongside the upstream side of Marble Hill House; its capacity was approximately 6-8 tons. There was certainly another, centrally placed, with a pond in the land between Orleans House and the Richmond Road, and another in the grounds of Lebanon House. There must have been others now long demolished and built over in the grounds of other large local 18th-century houses.

The availability of ice in the summer had always been a luxury but ice houses came into use and fashion only when Charles II brought the idea back from his exile in France. The appeal of ice was such that James II is recalled as having paid £1 a dish for ice cream. By the late 18th century no major house was without an ice house and they were built well into the 19th century. Refrigeration began in the 1850s and imports of ice had ceased by about 1910, but delivery of ice to various businesses continued until the last war.

THE GARDENS OF TWICKENHAM PARK

Francis Bacon, when he lived in Twickenham Park, 'found the situation of that place much convenient for the trial of my philosophical conclusions' and also created a celebrated garden there, but we have no details of this. However, when Lucy Harrington, Countess of Bedford, purchased the Park from him in 1608 for £1,800 she created another garden besides building a new house in the then fashionable brick. (Ham House followed a year later.) Robert Smythson, a mason/architect, many of whose houses and drawings survive, probably prepared the scale drawing of this house and garden as it was built. The garden was 321 ft. square bounded by a wall and within this were four hedges; the outer one was of quickthorn, cut as topiary in the shape of 'Beastes', and others of rosemary and fruit trees. Within these squares were concentric circles of birch, lime and fruit trees surrounding a circle of grass. In the corners between the circles and squares were mounts, or vantage points, reached by steps, possibly with small trees. The new

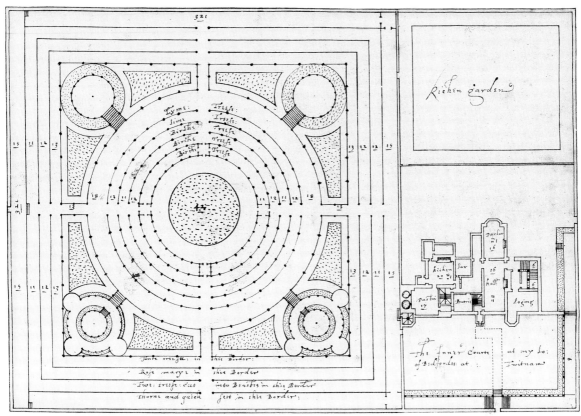

92. *Robert Smythson's plan of Twickenham Park House and Garden 1609.*
In the circles are 'Lyme' trees, Lime trees and three circles of Birch trees. Below, in the horizontal borders, are 'Fruite trees', 'Rose marye', 'Ewe trees cut with beastis', and 'Thorn and quick sett'. To the right is 'The inner courte at my Lords of Bedford at Twitnam'. Top right is the 'Kichen garden'.

house was alongside this on a plot about a quarter the size of the garden. Its position is known as it survived until the 19th century, and this places the garden at the southern end of today's ornamental lake (which originated as a drainage ditch in about 1420).

Daniel Langley, whose son Batty became a prolific writer on architectural and building matters, also worked on the Twickenham Park gardens between 1702 and 1726 when Thomas Vernon lived there. Several plane trees still in the St Margaret's estate grounds were planted by him. The largest had a height of 118 feet in 1983. In 1722 he converted a large sandpit in the Park 'then a perfect nuisance and supposed to be incapable of improvement', into a 'very agreeable beautiful' spiral garden perhaps 100 feet in diameter with hedges of hornbeam. He also spoke of a chestnut tree whose arms 'extend full four score feet'; and of the beautiful gardens embellished with hedges of hornbeam.

Other residents in the Park used it in different ways: for instance, the Duchess of Newcastle, in the 1760s, managed a wide variety of mixed farming; accounts were kept and even the house had to pay for produce taken.

The only later and detailed plan of the Park was when Francis Gosling owned it in 1817, but the 1608 house had gone by then and he lived in a house on the river bank at the end of what is now St Margaret's Drive. It was then a well-maintained estate with a 'capital walled kitchen garden, hot houses, Grapery and Pinery and succession houses', a 'Shrubbery Walk', a 'Wilderness and Ornamental Wood with stately cedar and forest trees', 'Flower Garden, Rosery and American Garden with a profusion of scarce and valuable plants'. With the house this was described as 'A Property almost Unique within the Distance from the Metropolis'

Whitton

KNELLER HALL

Two major estates were to dominate Whitton in the 18th century. In 1709 Sir Godfrey Kneller, the court painter, acquired a house in the centre of Whitton originally built by Edmund Cooke; this he demolished and he built a new one on the same site to his own plan, which included a hall and staircase painted by La Guerre with some assistance from the master. Kneller's marriage was childless but he did have a daughter, Agnes, from a liaison with a Mrs Voss; Agnes married a Mr Huckle and the child of that marriage, Godfrey Kneller Huckle, to whom Kneller became godfather, eventually inherited the estate in 1729, but didn't live there. The house in Kneller's lifetime was known as Whitton Hall, but ever since as Kneller Hall.

Huckle sold Kneller Hall in 1757 to Sir Samuel Prime, a prominent London lawyer. Laetitia Hawkins remembered him well: 'Though Sir Samuel was much too awful for my intimate observation, I regret that with him I lost an embodied idea of, I suppose, nearly the *costume* of Queen Anne's time; he wore a most voluminous wig, which yet, by the lightness of its curls, or I might almost say ringlets, seemed no heavier than the same quantity of smoke; it was, I suppose, though a little powdered, of the palest flaxen colour, corresponding with his really blooming complexion: his whole scale was large, but without any tendency to corpulency, his features were commanding, and his voice probably was pitched to Westminster Hall; it was extremely distinct, grave, and sonorous; his enunciation slow; and he began every sentence in addressing my father, with a 'Sir,' as profound as if he had addressed the House of Commons, by claiming of their Speaker.'

He lived at Kneller Hall until his death in 1777, when he was succeeded by his son, also Samuel and a lawyer, who much extended the Hall, and enlarged the grounds, including extending the pleasure grounds across the main road towards Twickenham; several houses opposite the Hall were pulled down to achieve this.

93. *'Whitton, Villa Godefridi Kneller', c1715; copper engraving by J. Kip.*

WHITTON PARK

The second estate developed in 18th-century Whitton was that of Archibald Campbell, Earl of Islay, later 3rd Duke of Argyll. In 1722 he bought the land enclosed out of the Heath by Henry Saunders in 1628-32, and with subsequent purchases he acquired a total of 55 acres. An active and unscrupulous politician, and virtual ruler of Scotland under Sir Robert Walpole, he was also keenly interested in the cultivation of rare plants. On his estate, which was enclosed by a moat, he grew exotic specimens, a tree nursery, and woodlands which included cedars, some of which still stand in the Old Latymerian's ground. He erected three buildings: a large stone greenhouse designed by James Gibbs, a house by Roger Morris, and a mock Gothic tower at the end of a long pond.

Much of the estate was sold to George Gostling in 1767 who divided the estate into two. The Argyll house and part of the land within the moat was leased out, firstly to Sir William Chambers the architect, who designed many of the buildings in Kew Gardens (including the Pagoda); the house was demolished after 1847. The greenhouse was converted into a mansion and there the Gostling family lived for the next 120 years. In 1892 the estate was sold for building though it was not until the mid 1930s that all the land was developed.

94. *Archibald, Duke of Argyll.*

95. *'A View of the Canal and of the Gothick Tower in the Garden of His Grace the Duke of Argyl'; painted and engraved by W. Woollett 1757. The Duke is seen on the left, wearing an apron, showing guests his estate.*

96. 'Whitton Place, the Seat of Sir Wm. Chambers'; copper engraving by Cary, c1790.

97. Whitton Park, lithograph by Stannard & Dixon, 1816; the house converted by G. Gostling from the Duke of Argyll's greenhouse.

98. *Sir William Chambers*

99. *The Earl of Bute*

WHITTON TREES FOR KEW

When the Duke of Argyll died in 1761 his nephew, the 3rd Earl of Bute, a keen botanist, was helping Augusta, Dowager Princess of Wales, to lay out her garden at Kew, which in due course became the Royal Botanic Gardens. In 1761/2 some of Argyll's finest trees and plants were transferred there. They included the following:

Sophora Japonica (Japanese Pagoda or Scholars Tree). First brought to England from Korea in 1753; this is now leaning over horizontally, but is well supported and still flowering.

Zelkova Carpinfolia (Caucasian Elm). One was blown down in the 1987 storm and a second lost in January 1990. There were probably three of these at Kew, presumably from the first introduction to England, planted at Whitton in 1760, though the survivor may be from a cutting, not an original.

Robinia Pseudacacia (False Acacia or Locust Tree).

This was first planted in England *c*1636.

Platinus Orientalis (Oriental Plane). The London Plane is a cross between this and the American Plane, which is rare in England. The cross probably arose in Spain about 1650. There are many large London Planes in Twickenham, mostly planted in the gardens and estates of the 18th-century wealthy; the first two were planted in Ely and at Barn Elms, across the river in Barnes.

Gingko Biloba (Maidenhair Tree). The single survivor of a family of trees in prehistoric times. This actual tree was the first to be grown in England, where it was raised from seed in the Mile End Nurseries in 1753 and sold to the Duke of Argyll in 1754.

All these trees are still growing near the Princess of Wales Conservatory, the Orangery and the Herbarium at the northern end of Kew Gardens, where Princess Augusta started her botanic garden.

Twickenham Drinking

INNS AND TAVERNS

The local inn has been a centre of social life in town and village for generations, though the nature of its use has been subject, at least in theory, to strict controls. A standard condition imposed by the Middlesex Justices in 1737 provided that publicans 'shall not Permit or Suffer any Playing at Cards Dice Tables Quoits Loggets Bowls or any other unlawful game or Games in his house outhouse Yard Garden or Backsides, Nor suffer any Person or Persons to become drunk or Remaining Tippling or Drinking therein contrary to Law nor suffer any other Disorders to be committed therein but do maintain Good Rule and Order therein.'

Public houses have, of all commercial properties, the longest tradition of operating from the same sites. In Twickenham a number of houses can trace their origins to the early 18th century. The Queen's Head can go back even earlier, and was probably serving the watermen of the river in the 17th century; it is

100. The White Swan Inn from a drawing by W. Luker Jnr. c1893, showing the name of Burrows and Cole.

101. Trade card of Mary Clarkson, licensee of the George Inn in 1775.

now known as the Barmy Arms, a longstanding local name for it. The most picturesque house on the river, the White Swan, formerly just the Swan, has been there since at least 1722. The Fox, formerly the Bell, in Church Street, is one pub that shows its age - the building probably dates from the time of Queen Anne. As one enters, the two steps down remind one that Church Street has risen over a foot since the place was built. The Black Dog in London Road is recorded as early as 1723; in recent years it has become a wine bar and trades under the name Twickers.

Cole's brewery near the present site of Twickenham station is shown in Glover's map of 1635, and the Cole family at one time owned some inns in Twickenham.

The White Hart at Whitton was probably the public house mentioned in the 1685 survey of public houses in Middlesex where a house with three beds and stabling for ten horses was mentioned. The Crown in Richmond Road was contemporary with the development of Montpelier Row; mentioned in 1730, it was run by a Catholic family, the Kilbournes, for the first 45 years, and owned by them late into the 18th century.

Two houses were developed in the 18th century to cater for the coach trade through King Street: The George (1737) and the King's Head (1747), opposite each other, were the two largest public houses in the parish in 1818; both had extensive yards for stabling, covering nearly a third of an acre each. The George, with the yard converted to a patio, is still there, but the old King's Head was demolished in 1926 when King Street was widened. A new King's Head was built in the garden behind and opened when the road was completed, but in its latter years declined in popularity, and after a brief spell as a pub for young people, the Bird's Nest, closed and has been replaced by a restaurant.

The Eel Pie Island Hotel, once extremely popular, has also gone: its history is described on pp79-80. The

102. *Cover of* The Bloudy booke *showing Sir John Fitz stabbing himself after killing Daniel Alley, landlord of the Anchor Inn in Twickenham and wounding his wife, in August 1605.*

103. King Street, showing the King's Head on the left, and the George (on the right with bay windows). Lithograph by James Gooch c1832.

present Duke's Head, in Albion Road, dates from 1914; it replaced an earlier building which was on a site slightly to the south, with a frontage on Colne Road. Originally this was on the main road across the heath to Staines, before enclosures diverted the road a little to the south. It had a large bay window from which the comings and goings could be seen, and like all the pubs on the heath it has its highwayman story. It is claimed that whilst hiding from constables, Dick Turpin carved his initials on the cellar door of the pub, though it seems unlikely that the constables would fail to search the cellars.

The Red Lion, in Heath Road, another 18th-century house, would also have been on the edge of Hounslow Heath; it was rebuilt this century. The present buildings of the Royal Oak on the corner of Oak Lane (first known in 1723 and now called the Hedgehog and Stump), and the Three Kings (1731) in Heath Road, occupy the sites of the old pubs.

About twenty public houses are recorded in Twickenham in the first third of the 18th century, but in 1737 the Middlesex magistrates, alarmed at 'the immodest drinking of Geneva and other distilled spirituous liquors', required constables to be more

energetic in making sure all premises selling liquor were licensed. This resulted in thirty-six premises being licensed that year. Later, the number declined and by 1760 they were down to twenty-three, falling to twenty by 1800. This was due to the centralisation of trade in a few of the larger premises.

The population increase of the early 19th century was not matched by an increase in the number of pubs. The Prince Blucher opened in 1815, but was counterbalanced by the closure of the Post Boy in London Road. It was a change in the law that provided an impetus for more public houses. The Beer Act of 1830 permitted any householder to sell beer and cider after obtaining a licence from the Commissioners of Excise; many of the beer shops opened then and some became fully-fledged public houses. The Admiral Nelson, Whitton, was one of the first of these, with the Rifleman in Fourth Cross Road, Turk's Head in Winchester Road, and the Five Oaks and Sussex Arms in Staines Road following.

As Twickenham expanded along the main roads new pubs were opened, such as the Rising Sun in Richmond Road (by 1847), the Prince of Wales along Hampton Road (1870), and the Pope's Grotto in

Cross Deep (1853). The Grotto was demolished by a flying bomb in 1944, but later rebuilt on a different part of the same site. Three pubs opened with the coming of the railway: the Albany Hotel, the Railway Hotel (since demolished) and the Railway Tavern (now the Cabbage Patch).

By 1900 the number of houses had risen to 35 with 30 beer shops in addition. In the 20th century came the Winning Post on the new Chertsey Road, and the Fountain in Staines Road; these were laid out with large car parks and in this respect were the equivalent of the old coaching inns.

LOCAL WINE CELLARS
In the late 1760s the Duchess of Newcastle produced only one or two bottles of port to drink at each dinner and supper at what became Twickenham Park. Her cellar, at Twickenham at any rate, was probably modestly stocked. But the owner of the house in 1817, Francis Gosling, a banker, was a heavier drinker and when the contents of his cellar were sold at auction after his death, they revealed a larger stock than the Duchess would have had. Gosling had 124 bottles of sherry, 147 bottles of Madeira and no less than 720 bottles of port. This may seem excessive, but when the owner of Gordon House, General Thomas Bland, died in 1816, his cellar contained 949 bottles of port, 192 of sherry, 221 of Madeira as well as good stocks of claret and Malaga.

104. The Admiral Nelson Inn, Whitton, decorated for the Coronation of George V, 1911.

Early Suburbia

POPULATION TRENDS

In the 19th century precise details of the population became available for the first time. Births, deaths and marriages began to be listed in church registers in 1538, but to extract a clear picture of population from these is difficult and time consuming. The Hearth Tax Returns in the 1660s, by giving details of the number of hearths in each house, enable the size of each household to be calculated. However, the first proper Census was carried out in 1801 though the name of each individual in a household was not recorded until 1841. The Census has taken place at ten-yearly intervals ever since, except in the war year of 1941.

In Twickenham and Whitton the population increased from just over 3,000 in 1801 to approximately 21,000 in 1901; it peaked at 52,564 in 1951, but had

105. The heart of Twickenham in 1860; King Street, showing the George Inn on the left, and Page's draper's shop at the far end. This was demolished when York Street was built at the end of the century to allow for more traffic to Richmond than was possible through Church Street, the sole former route.

106. *Trafalgar Square (now Trafalgar Road) was built in the 1840s. This photograph shows a pair of double-fronted semi-detached houses.*

107. *The official opening of York Street ,1 March 1899; in the carriage are Henry Little, Chairman of the U.D.C., County Councillor Dr M.C. Ward, Ralph Littler, Chairman of Middlesex County Council, and James Bigwood, MP for Brentford (which then included Twickenham).*

fallen away to 40,577 in 1981. The 1871 Census first recorded in a detailed way the occupations of residents. We find that of a working population of 4646 (men and women), about 400 were engaged in agriculture, 600 in manufacture, 542 in 'dealing', 541 were professionals or in public service, and over 1600 were in domestic service.

SHARING OUT THE LAND

It was not until 1818 that the large amount of common land in Twickenham was shared out and enclosed. It went to local landowners in proportion to what they already held, and there were provisions in the Act for the forming of new roads, the laying of public drains, and the erection of fencing. It was this Act which allowed the development of the town and parish.

The improvement of transport later in the 19th century was equally important to development. Canals had been introduced into the area at the end of the 18th century (there were locks at Teddington in 1811), and this had the effect of increasing river traffic, with barge and wharf business below St Mary's church and along the embankment. But the arrival of the railway across the river from Richmond in 1850 was more significant - by 1871 there were already 94 railway employees living here - because it allowed for convenient commuting to London. Road transport increased and although the car did not appear before the early years of the 20th century, York Street was opened in 1899 to provide a wider route to Richmond than Church Street.

GORDON HOUSE AND LACY HOUSE

Gordon House acquired its name after 1836 when Lord George, and after him Lord Frederick, Gordon lived there. The first house on the site was built about 1437 for a keeper of Twickenham Park, '...a dwelling consisting of a hall, kitchen and chambers with a little garden annexed...'. In 1635 Mr Gimmer, the Rector at Isleworth, lived there and his neighbour was Thomas Willis, 'Gent y Schole', the schoolmaster of Isleworth.

The present Gordon House is difficult to follow architecturally. The central entrance section facing the river was built about 1717 for Moses Hart, a stockbroker; the architect is unkown but may have been Thomas Archer, who designed St John's church in Smith Square, Westminster. The staircase inside was made by Nicholas Dubois, a former Army engineer, who later took up architecture and building. (This staircase was probably the prototype of the well-known flying staircase at Chevening House in Kent.) The upstream block of the house was the first that Robert Adam built in England; his client was General Humphrey Bland, a distinguished soldier, whose widow lived on here until 1816. The main room is magnificent and follows almost in full Adam's drawings now in the Sir John Soane Museum in London. The date of the downstream wing of the house is not known but inside it has 17th and 18th century mouldings and other features. The garden front of the house is of a single architectural style, of uncertain date.

At about the time Adam designed his part of Gordon House in 1758, he also 'designed and ex-

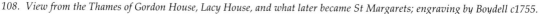

108. View from the Thames of Gordon House, Lacy House, and what later became St Margarets; engraving by Boydell c1755.

ecuted a Green House to a classical design' (at this time glass roofs had not yet become practicable). Adam's heading on this drawing indicated that a similar Green House was also to be built for Sir Nathaniel Curzon (1675-1758), presumably at Kedleston, of which he was the 4th Baronet. The precise situation of this in the Gordon House garden has not yet been established. At the same time Adam designed a Temple, but this may not have been built.

Lacy House was built about 1750 by James Lacy, co-manager with David Garrick of Drury Lane Theatre. In the 1780s Sir Edward Walpole, the elder brother of Horace, lived there. The house was finally demolished in the 1820s.

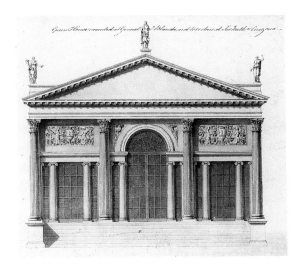

109. (Right) Robert Adam's design for a Green House for General Bland, Gordon House..

110. (Below) Lacy House; engraving by Spencer 1775.

ST MARGARET'S HOUSE

By 1851 the Classic period of Twickenham had passed and the nobility and wealthy of Marble Hill and Twickenham Park and elsewhere along the river had moved on. There was now pressure in Twickenham to develop the old estates.

A late resident of Twickenham Park, until 1817, was the banker, Francis Gosling, a partner of Gosling & Sharpe, who were absorbed by Barclays Bank at the end of the century - 'Gosling's' branch of Barclays is still at 11 Fleet Street. The next owner, the Earl of Cassilis (later the Marquis of Ailsa), renamed his estate St Margaret's in about 1820, and by 1850 this name had begun to be used for the area and by 1860 it was in the Twickenham rate books: it was finally confirmed as a local place name in 1872 when the railway station opened.

It is interesting that in 1439 the boundaries of Twickenham and Isleworth were defined with about half the Park falling into each parish. In 1992 the Boundary Commission recommended that the whole of the old Park, from the river Crane to the south and east should be joined to Twickenham so that the old Park area is united under one authority.

By 1840 development had begun within the Park with the erection of some substantial villas such as Willoughby House near Richmond Bridge, Ryde House in Richmond Road, and Park and Bute Lodges in Park Road.

Early in the 1850s the Earl of Kilmorey, the new owner of the estate, built a new St Margaret's House at a cost of £16,920; it was designed by Lewis Vulliamy and built by William Cubitt. However, Kilmorey decided that he could not afford to live there and all the land up to the railway was sold in 1854 to the Conservative Land Society. The house and part of the land became the Royal Naval Female School, which had been founded in Richmond in 1840. Unfortunately, the house was destroyed by a bomb in September 1940.

111. St Margaret's (the second) from the river; drawn and engraved by Frederick Smith 1832.

112. *Caen Lodge (later Willoughby House); engraving by Cooke, c1851.*

113. *St Margaret's (the third), built in 1852; engraving by Laing, 1852.*

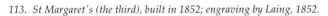

PHIZ AND BOZ IN TWICKENHAM

Towards the end of the residence of the Marquis of Ailsa in Twickenham Park, in the 1830s, part of his land was redeveloped by the building of Ailsa Park Villas, about ten houses, between what became the railway and the St Margaret's roundabout. Charles Dickens ('Boz') lived in no. 2 in the summer months of 1838, and there wrote part of *Oliver Twist* and some of *Nicholas Nickleby*, parts of which are set in Petersham. He 'had many friendly days' here with Thackeray, Douglas Jerrold, Landseer and Maclise as his guests. Fortunately, no. 2 survived when the remainder of these houses were destroyed during the last war.

Some scenes illustrated by Hablot Knight Browne ('Phiz') in *Little Dorrit* (1857) are set in Twickenham, where the Meagles have a house 'on a road by the river...Within view was the peaceful river and the ferry-boat'. During his visit Clennam crosses the river by the ferry, and on his return along the towing path, finds Henry Gowan, later his successful rival for Pet's hand, sitting with his dog awaiting the ferry.

114. *2 Ailsa Park Villas. Photograph by Alan Urwin*

115. *The Ferry. Illustration to Dickens'* Little Dorrit, *1857.*

THE ELMS, DUCKS WALK

This house was built just after the railway crossed the river in 1850. Its garden is still laid out as it was in 1863 and is at the original level of the land, while Ducks Walk was raised; eventually a river wall was built to keep out high tides. Starting as a 'Gentleman's residence', the house later took in 'City Gentlemen as Paying Guests'. It is now one of the properties split up into small flats by the Richmond Churches Housing Trust.

EEL PIE ISLAND

Formerly known as Twickenham Ait, this island figured in the early history of Twickenham, but was perhaps more notable as the first site for public entertainment in the parish. Glover's map of 1635 indicates that the central plot of just over an acre 'hath bin A Boulding Alley'. There has been an inn on the island since at least 1737, initially called the Ship, and later the White Cross on the Ayte. The old premises, described as 'a dingy wooden cottage', were replaced in 1830 by a building on a much grander scale, capable of accommodating parties of nearly two hundred. During the 19th century it was a popular resort for boating parties on summer afternoons. In *Nicholas Nickleby* (1839), Dickens tells

116. The Elms. Photograph by Alan Urwin

117. Eel Pie Island. Pen and watercolour by Thomas Rowlandson

118. *Twickenham Ait. Lithograph by J. Gooch 1832. Eel Pie Island is in the foreground; St Mary's church, on the farther shore, is to the right.*

us: 'It had come to pass, that afternoon, that Miss Morleena Kenwigs had received an invitation to repair next day, per steamer from Westminster Bridge, unto the Eel-pie Island at Twickenham: there to make merry upon a cold collation, bottled-beer, shrub and shrimps, and to dance in the open air to the music of a locomotive band.' However, even in the 19th century, Francis Francis noted the decline in the eel population which furnished the delicacy and gave the island its name. Despite this, the hotel continued into the twentieth century, with music on summer evenings and a vocalist singing from the balcony. But recreational patterns changed, and in the 1950s there were few boating visitors and the hotel was losing money. It was saved by becoming a club for popular and jazz music in 1957 and in the 'sixties many groups, including the Rolling Stones and Black Sabbath played there. The building was becoming derelict by 1970 and the refusal of the magistrates to renew the drinking licence meant the end of it. In 1971 it burnt down during demolition and houses now occupy the site.

MEADOWBANK AND GEORGE BISHOP'S OBSERVATORY

Meadowbank and its thirty acres of land were sold in 1861 to John Parson, a property developer. Almost immediately he sold the house and nine acres to a Mr George Bishop, whose father had recently died. The late George Bishop had been a noted astronomer, in the front rank of amateurs, and at one time was President of the Royal Astronomical Society. Several major discoveries were made from his observatory in Regent's Park, but recently there had been 'frequent interruption from the lights and smoke of London' and so in 1863 the younger George removed his father's instruments and valuable library to the recently completed observatory which had been built in the grounds of his new house in Twickenham, on 'a site possessing a very open view of the southern heavens'.

The position of this observatory had been carefully determined astronomically and geodetically with the assistance of the Director-General of the Ordnance Survey, Sir Henry James. The Equatorial room containing the instruments measured fifteen feet in diameter with a dome rising to eighteen feet six inches, and the observing chair gained for his maker the medal of the Society of Arts. A transit room, library, sleeping apartment and storage room completed the building.

George Bishop sold Meadowbank in 1877 for £14,000 and retired to France after presenting the instruments and other apparatus to the Royal Observatory at Naples. The house then changed hands several times, and according to local gossip, was one of several houses rented by Lily Langtry, the actress and mistress of Edward VII. However, it was purchased in 1919 by the Eastern Telegraph Company (now Cable & Wireless) for use as 'The Exiles Club' for their overseas employees. The observatory was demolished in 1961/2 and the present clubhouse opened in 1963.

119. Mr Bishop's Observatory, Meadowbank 1869.

120. Interior of Mr Bishop's Observatory 1869.

121. *Sandycombe Lodge; engraving by Cooke after Havell, 1814.*

TURNER AT SANDYCOMBE LODGE

Originally called Solus Lodge, this house is still almost just as it was when built by the landscape artist, J.M.W. Turner. He bought the land here in 1807; he liked and knew the river well as he had spent some time at school at Brentford. Then, acting as his own foreman and from sketches in his pocket books now in the British Museum, and with much care, he built his house between 1810 and 1813. Its appearance from the garden side is shown in the illustration above. It had much more land than it does now, stretching along St Margaret's Road about half way towards the present traffic lights at Richmond Road, and had views from the upper rooms to Richmond Hill and the river. He made a square pond at the bottom of the garden which was 'planted by him so thickly with willows that his father...complained that it was a mere osier bed'. Twickenham was a place for relaxation where he enjoyed his favourite sport of fishing and his garden, but he did not spend much time here, continually travelling between London and Twickenham..

Turner's friend from boyhood, Henry Scott Trimmer, vicar of Heston, recalled the house:

'It was an unpretending little place, and the rooms were small. There were several models of ships in glass cases, to which Turner had painted a sea and background. They much resembled the large vessels in his sea pieces. Richmond scenery greatly influ-

ences his style. The Scotch firs (or stone-pine) around are in most of his classical subjects, and Richmond landscape is decidedly the basis of *The Rise of Carthage.*'

Henry's son, Frederick, also recalled:

'I have dined with him at Sandycombe Lodge, when my father happened to drop in too, in the middle of the day. Everything was of the most modest pretensions, two-pronged forks, and knives with large round ends for taking up the food; not what I ever saw him so use them, though it is said to have been Dean Swift's mode of feeding himself. The tablecloth barely covered the table, the earthenware was in strict keeping. I remember him saying one day, "Old dad," as he called his father, "have you not any wine?" whereupon Turner, senior, produced a bottle of currant, at which Turner, smelling, said: "Why, what have you been about?" The senior, it seemed, had rather overdone it with hollands, and it was set aside. At this time Turner was a very abstemious person.'

Turner senior, a keen gardener and lover of birds, fought an unending war with the local boys who went bird nesting. They in turn called him 'Old Blackbird'. The old man also went up most days to London to look after his son's gallery, hitching a lift in the carts of the local market gardeners, who sent produce up to town. As for Turner himself, on Wednesday 7 July 1819 he went up river in the Ordnance shallop lent by the Duke of Wellington.

122. *Sketch of J.M.W. Turner in later life.*

The boat contained ten rowers and eleven artists, in a procession of city barges and river boats. At Barnes the travellers had bread and cheese. They reached Eel Pie Island at about 3pm and sat down to eat at 4pm.

Turner sold the house in 1826 because of his father's continual colds. A small part of the garden remains at the original ground level, the remainder having been built on later in the century. The house has remained in private occupation since.

THE CONSERVATIVE LAND SOCIETY

This Society was formed in 1852 to exploit the idea of building societies, which themselves dated from 1775, and the 1832 Reform Act. The general idea, initiated by the Liberals in Birmingham in 1847, was to purchase estates and develop them so that the residents could become registered voters in the interests of the party concerned. The Conservative Land Society purchased estates in Kentish Town, Maldon, Maidstone, Brighton and Taunton. In Twickenham the Society developed the St Margaret's estate which, from its spacious layout and fourteen acres of communal gardens, was similar in concept to the garden suburbs of Letchworth, Bedford Park, Welwyn and Hampstead. The ornamental lake in one of the grounds dates from the drainage ditch dug for the nuns of Syon monastery shortly after 1415.

Within two or three years of the purchase of the estate in 1854 the familiar names of Ailsa, St Peter's, Cassilis and Heathcote Roads and The Avenue, had appeared - St George's Road was originally called Park Road. The price of the 272 planned plots varied from £50 in Heathcote Road to £475 at the river end of The Avenue. The Society's aim of expanding the franchise allowed under the Reform Act was achieved very quickly with a very wide spread of owners, describing themselves as esquires, gentlemen, bankers, chemists, dentists, boot and shoe makers, wine merchants, gardeners, architects, etc. Only a few of them were local people. By 1857, when the 18th quarterly meeting of the Society was held, land had been sold to the value of £203,046.

By buying these plots the owners were enfranchised and, of course, were almost obliged to vote Conservative. After the 1857 General Election the Society reported that all but 8% of the members had voted appropriately. But the plot owners had still to build their own houses. Most did so, but over a period of many years, hence the variety of architectural styles. Some owners did not build, and even forgot about their plots, which resulted in the number of houses now with double plots acquired by rights of occupation.

123. St Margaret's Estate as planned by the Conservative Land Society. The church shown was never built. Poster of 1854.

JAMES GOOCH

James Gooch was something of a Pooh-Bah in 19th-century Twickenham; apart from his main office of Vestry Clerk, to which he was appointed at a salary of £20 in 1833, he was Registrar of Births and Deaths, Census Registrar from 1841 to 1861, Collector of Rates, Assistant Overseer of the Poor, and Clerk to the Highways Board. He was also Clerk to the Tithes Commissioners in 1845.

His main interest, however, is in his artistic work. He came from Norfolk, a pupil of John Crome, and apart from some paintings, executed five lithographs in 1832 which give us our first glimpse of the *village* of Twickenham as opposed to its great houses. One is of Twickenham Ait (Eel Pie Island) with St Mary's church in the background; the other four, sometimes found printed on a single sheet, show streets in Twickenham, and with carts, beasts of burden, a herd of cattle, and various pedestrians, giving a vivid impression of life in those more leisured days.

Gooch retired at the age of 76 in 1867 and settled in Queen Street with an unmarried daughter, herself a landscape painter. He died five years later.

Reproduced here are three of his views; two others are on pages 69 and 80.

124. London Road looking south; this view, from the approximate position of the bus stop, shows a hay cart emerging from Shews Lane (now Amyand Park Road), with the road in the distance leading to what is now the Junction.

125. *Church Street looking west; taken from the corner of the churchyard, this depicts, on the left, the buildings on the corner of Church Lane, a site now occupied by Church Square. To the right are the gates of the Manor House.*

126. *King Street looking east; the George is to the left; the right-hand side of the road shows some of the shops which were swept away when it was widened in the 1920s, and the Parish beadle can be seen in his uniform on the right.*

'THE TWICKENHAM FRONT GARDEN' OF BUCCLEUGH HOUSE

Buccleugh House was situated on the lawns between Petersham Road and the river, just below today's Terrace Gardens in Richmond; only the mews and the outhouses remain at the bottom of the Terrace. The main gardens of the house were sold to Richmond Vestry for a public open space in the 1890s and became the Terrace Gardens; the Buccleugh House grounds that were left were therefore small.

Sir John Whittaker Ellis, MP and former Lord Mayor of London, and also mayor of Richmond in 1890/1, solved the problem of his restricted garden in 1896 by purchasing Cambridge Park House on the Twickenham side of the river, next to Meadowbank and its observatory. The meadowland which stretched from the formal gardens fronting the house to the river was transformed into pleasure grounds for Sir John, his family and guests, who were rowed across the river to sample them. Described as having been 'laid out at very great cost being one of the best specimens of modern landscape gardening in the neighbourhood and forming a most delightful source of amusement and recreation', the grounds had spacious lawns, and walks terminating in vistas containing statuary. An Italian garden with an ornamental fountain near the centre, tennis and croquet lawns, and a bowling green, completed the attractions.

Quite the most extravagant gesture was the demolition of the existing house, to be replaced by a very large conservatory using the same foundations. Forming part of this new building was a 'Garden House comprising capital reception rooms, with ornamental fireplace and statuary marble chimney piece; large Cloakrooms and expensively fitted up Lavatories having Hot and Cold water supplies'.

In the 1930s this garden house and the conservatory became the site of Cambridge Park Court and the Old Garden.

WHITTON IN THE 19TH CENTURY

A major change was to affect Whitton in 1818. Hounslow Heath was enclosed by Act of Parliament and as new roads were laid out across the old heath Whitton was extended to twice its old area. Though roads such as Hounslow and Percy Roads (following old edges of cultivated land) and Nelson and Hospital Bridge Roads, and Powder Mill Lane, were planned, actual building was slow, and Whitton was a relatively isolated village still.

When the owner of Kneller Hall, Samuel Prime jnr, died in 1813 his house was sold to Charles Calvert, member of a wealthy brewing family and a Whig Member of Parliament for Southwark. He expanded the house under the supervision of Philip Hardwick (architect of Euston Station), adding two wings on to Kneller's original house. The Government acquired the building in 1847 to use as a training school for schoolmasters who were to teach pauper and criminal children. The walls and timbers of Kneller's house were found to be dilapidated and this part was taken down and a new central bock was added by George Mair, based on Wollaston Hall. The sections added by Charles Calvert formed the wings of the new house.

The Hall was opened as a Training School in 1850 with Dr Frederick Temple as Principal and Francis Turner Palgrave as vice-principal, but the school was not a success and it was closed in 1856. The Hall was then acquired by the War Department as a School to teach army bandsmen. This was just at the end of the Crimean War when it had been noticeable that the bands in the army regiments were mainly filled by German musicians and it was felt that native bandsmen should be trained. So, the School was opened as the Military School of Music on 3 March 1857 and thirty years later added 'Royal' to its title. It has a worldwide reputation, attracting students from all

127. *Conservatory, Cambridge Park House.*

128. *Kneller Hall from a drawing by pupils of Mr Gittins' School, 1851.*

129. *Band of the Royal Military School of Music, Kneller Hall, c1900.*

130. *St Philip and St James church, Whitton; from a postcard.*

parts of the world, especially from the Commonwealth. Soon after its opening Kneller Hall began a series of summer open-air concerts, giving the pupil musicians a chance to play to a live audience and also providing local residents with musical entertainment. These concerts continue to the present day, and on some occasions 5,000 people have attended, almost enough to fill the Albert Hall.

Most of the housing of the village developed during the 19th century was small-scale and usually for working families, or were small villas. The church of St Philip and St James, on land donated by the Gostling family of Whitton Park, was erected in 1862, and there were two public houses, the White Hart in Kneller Road, which still trades, and the Red Lion in Nelson Road, which has been replaced by a row of houses.

Whitton had one moment of notoriety when, in 1869, a local dignitary called Louis Kyezor was murdered. Kyezor, a wealthy financier, had settled in Whitton in the 1850s and had built a number of working-class houses - one row in Hounslow Road and another in Nelson Road still survive. A dispute

131. *Bell Lane; watercolour by E.B. Phipson 1904.*

132. Photograph of the Mission Room (now Mary Wallace Theatre) by D.H. Simpson 1990.

arose with one of his tenants, Thomas Green, over the state of Green's cottage and Kyezor ordered his eviction. One morning in October 1869 Green waited for Kyezor in Hounslow Road and shot him in the stomach. Green then rushed back to his own cottage, and in the privy at the bottom of the garden shot himself in the head. Both men died.

The story achieved national prominence as it was thought that Green was in fact George Edwards, the man who had informed on the Cato Street conspiracy in 1820. A number of speculative theories as to the reason for the murder were put forward in the press, but it was only a thirteen-day wonder. It had just been the action of an irascible and angry old man.

THE DARKER SIDE OF HOUSING

For many years the area between Church Street and the river, the oldest inhabited part of Twickenham, had become run down and overcrowded and conditions did not greatly improve until the 20th century. In 1851 one small tenement in Church Alley housed fifteen people.

One measure to alleviate poverty, particularly in the hard winters, was the parish Soup Kitchen. This was in use as early as 1861, and in 1893 it was transferred to a special building at the rear of the Mission Room. This Room (now the Mary Wallace Theatre) was built near the riverside in 1870 to help those thought to be in need both materially and spiritually; there was an emphasis on thrift clubs, sewing circles, literacy and temperance. Despite its efforts, the vicar of Twickenham, the Rev. H.F. Limpus, wrote in his parish magazine in 1875:

'There is another subject that is very near to my heart and about which I feel very strongly...I refer to the dwellings of the poor. We may collect funds - we may enlarge our schools, - we may enlist admirable teachers, we may obtain a council of education...but it will be all in vain, most utterly in vain so long as the poor are doomed to be huddled together in their present dwellings. The home influence is always the strongest and whatever impression may be produced in schools must of necessity be destroyed in such homes as many of the children are obliged to return to. Not one wealthy man would allow his cattle to be housed in such places as I could point out to him'. After quoting a hovel of two rooms containing a family of six, with another child expected, he pleaded for swift change. 'Then we might sweep away forever the block of sheds and hovels extending from the Church down to Water Lane.'

French Royals

THE ORLEANS PRINCES IN TWICKENHAM

In 1800, three brothers came to live in Twickenham. They had all been keen supporters of the French Revolution, the oldest having fought in the revolutionary armies. But after years of exile or imprisonment in a squalid Marseilles prison, the brothers sought shelter in England. They were short of funds and moved into a modest house called Highshot, in Crown Road. The eldest was Louis Philippe Duc d'Orleans, and the younger were Antoine Duc de Montpensier, and Louis Charles Comte de Beaujolais. They spent the next seven years based in Twickenham accompanied by a few followers and servants who included an English valet, George White. They were friends of the Duke of Kent and with the Austrian Ambassador then living at York House. In 1807, Montpensier died of tuberculosis, a consequence of his time in prison. Louis Philippe removed his youngest brother out of England but Beaujolais also died in the following year. Nevertheless, Louis Philippe had a strong affection for Twickenham as indeed had his brothers: 'good old Twick', 'dear quiet Twick'. So when Napoleon made his attempt at a comeback in 1815, Louis Philippe returned to the safety of this place, but since he was now married and had a family he chose to reside in Orleans House. There he set up a printing press for his children (run by his old valet, George White). After Napoleon's defeat at Waterloo the duc remained in Twickenham for another two years; during that time a daughter was born, who was christened in St Mary's. When he returned to France in the spring of 1817 his furnishings and heavy luggage were shipped down the Thames by barge.

Louis Philippe became King of the French in 1830 and was dethroned in 1848, dying at Claremont House, Esher in 1851. Before his death he visited Twickenham on two more occasions: in October 1844, when on a state visit to England, and shortly after his dethronement when staying temporarily at a hotel on Richmond Hill. On that occasion he met an old acquaintance, the former landlord of the Crown

133. Highshot House; lithograph of c1817.

134. *Visit of Louis Philippe, King of the French, to Orleans House, 1844. Lithograph by Pringret 1846.*

135. *The Duke of Orleans c1900*

136. *King Manoel and Queen Augusta c1914.*

137. *Fulwell Park; the name possibly derives from a local Full or Foul Well.*

Inn in Richmond Road, who greeted the ex-King by reminding him that 'he had kept the Crown'. Louis Philippe dryly remarked that that was more than he had managed to do.

Four generations of Louis Philippe's descendants at one time or another lived in Twickenham. Their heyday was in the 1860s when three of his sons resided in the vicinity: the Duc d'Aumale at Orleans House, the Prince de Joinville at Lebanon House and the Duc de Nemours at Bushy Park. In addition two of his grandsons lived close at hand: the Comte de Paris at York House and his brother, the Duc de Chartres, across the river at Morgan House.

Although the princes returned to France in 1871, their ties with Twickenham were not totally broken. In 1895, one of the Comte de Paris' daughters was married to the Italian Duke of Aosta and the wedding breakfast took place at Orleans House. The old Duc d'Aumale was present. Then, in 1896, York House was purchased and greatly enlarged by the Comte's only son, now himself Duc d'Orleans. Signs of his stay are still evident all over the building in the form of *fleur de lys* decorations or symbolic French Crowns. In 1899 a reception was held at York House for another royal wedding, that of the youngest sister of the Duc d'Orleans to her first cousin, Jean Duc de Guise. The Duc d'Orleans moved away from Twickenham in

1900 but did not sell his house here until 1906. He and his sister - they had both been born here - paid a last one-day visit to their old home in 1903.

The sister, Marie Amelie d'Orleans, had married into the Portuguese royal family - her husband and then her second son were both kings of Portugal. But a revolution in 1910 expelled the young king Manoel and he and his mother fled to England. They lived at first in Richmond, but on marrying, Manoel settled down to live in Fulwell Park, Twickenham. He supported local groups such as the Cottage Garden Society and the local Piscatorial Society, and he was a prominent figure at the Twickenham Charter Day ceremonies in 1926. His motor car, a Rolls Royce, was regularly serviced at Orleans Garage in Richmond Road.

Manoel died in July 1932 aged only 42. The funeral cortège from Westminster Cathedral to Weybridge passed through Twickenham, where the streets were lined by schoolchildren. He had been a keen supporter of St James' church, Pope's Grove, having presented it with communion plate, a church organ, and a memorial window to St Antony of Padua (the window bears the family crest).

Mementos of the Orleans princes are to be found today in street names, or in the names and decorations of buildings locally: Orleans Road, School, Gations of buildings locally: Orleans Road, School, Garage and House, Portugal Gardens, D'Aumale Cottages, Manoel Road, Augusta Road and Lisbon Avenue. Nearly all the houses that they lived in have disappeared, but one curious relic of King Manoel has survived: the four-ton safe that used to store the royal jewellery at Fulwell Park, is now housed in St Mary's church, Hampton.

A CARTOUCHE IN RIVERSIDE HOUSE

Pictured here is a large carved stone, shield shaped cartouche in the garden of Riverside House. It is surmounted by a ducal crown and incorporates a cipher with the interlaced initials 'H.O.'. It is unlike the design of coats of arms that we are accustomed to see in England. It is French in style and can only have been executed for Henri Duc d'Aumale for the decoration of his English house, which became Orleans House: he lived there between 1854 and 1863. This is probably the only one remaining of several examples on the walls of the house and its attached buildings.

THE DE VIDIL CASE

Another Twickenham French connection was headline news. In June 1861, a Frenchman, the Baron de Vidil (who, though an Orleanist supporter, had no direct connection with the royal exiles), was accused of attempting to murder his own son in the roadway running from the White Swan to Orleans House, by striking him over the head with a heavy riding whip. The Baron was arrested in France as a result of a sworn deposition made by his son before Bow Street magistrates, but later, when the case came for trial, he refused to give evidence against his father and as a result the son was sent to prison for a month. The Baron was convicted on the lesser charge of wounding and given one year's hard labour.

The case aroused wide interest in the national and local press. Several of the witnesses were local. Some had been at the Swan when the wounded man was brought in, and another witness gave a dying deposition from his bed in Sion Cottages. But the case was full of unsolved mysteries. Some thought the Baron was after his son's fortune (derived from his English mother and her relatives); other evidence pointed to the son's mental instability: though he had taken a First at Cambridge he had also spent time in a private asylum.

138. *Cartouche, Riverside House. Photograph by Alan Urwin.*
139. *Baron de Vidil*

Local Enterprise

LOCAL GOVERNMENT AND LIBRARIES

The first representative body in Twickenham concerned with local affairs was the Select Vestry of sixteen members, with the vicar and churchwardens *ex officio*, set up on the order of the Bishop of London in 1618; its minutes, preserved in the church archives and available in microfiche in Richmond Library, record, together with the churchwardens' accounts dating from 1606, the diverse topics which these local worthies discussed. There were, of course, church affairs - the repair of the building, the allocation of pews and vaults, the care of the bells: the ringing of bells on public occasions is a reminder of the close links between church and community. Education, including the election of pupils to Christ's Hospital in the City, highways and bridges, the parish bull, public order and the provision of stocks for malefactors, the care of the poor, the establishment of almshouses and workhouses, the provision of fire engines - these are just some of the subjects covered. In later years a Lighting Committee and a Highways Committee carried out some of the detailed work.

The Poor Law Act of 1834 transferred the care of the poor to Boards of Guardians, but a greater change came with the passage of the Local Government Act of 1858. This provided for the setting up of local Boards of Health, whose scope was much wider than their title suggested. Their establishment was, however, voluntary and depended on a poll of ratepayers. Twickenham was slower than neighbouring villages to adopt the Act; it was eventually discussed towards the end of 1867, endorsed by a poll and the first meeting of the Board was in February 1868. The powers of the Vestry were much diminished by the Board's establishment and were then further eroded so that it became a purely church body.

The Board's offices were in Queen's Road, but in 1877 the property developer, Charles Freake, who developed much of Brompton, built a Town Hall with an auditorium at the rear and smaller rooms at the front, some of which he allowed the Board to use. This situation continued when the Board of Health became an Urban District Council in 1895.

The Town Hall also housed the first public library in Twickenham. A meeting was held in December 1881 which agreed to adopt the Public Libraries Act and this was confirmed by a poll - Twickenham was the first public authority in Middlesex outside the London area to take this step. Two rooms in the Town Hall, to which a third was later added, were

140. *Laying the Foundation Stone of the Public Library, Garfield Road, 18 June 1906.*

141. *The Old Town Hall, King Street.*

142. *Charter Day, 22 September 1926. The change of status from Urban District Council to Borough was an occasion of great rejoicing in Twickenham. This photograph, taken at Denton Road, East Twickenham, shows the Charter Mayor, Dr. J.R. Leeson, with Town Clerk, Edwin Stray and Deputy Clerk, F.H. Stollard on his right, and Brentford MP and Home Secretary, Sir William Joynson Hicks on his left.*

allocated for the library, but by the early years of this century these were inadequate and an approach was made to the great benefactor of libraries, Andrew Carnegie, who agreed to provide a building for Twickenham. This was in Garfield Road; the foundation stone was laid in 1906 and the Library opened the following year. Though much altered internally, the building is still in use.

In 1926 Twickenham became a borough, and in the same year a new Town Hall was opened. The front portion of the old building was marked for demolition in the proposed widening of King Street and the UDC, soon to become a borough council, purchased York House as a Town Hall. In 1937 the Borough of Twickenham was enlarged to bring in the neighbouring Urban Districts of Hampton, Hampton Wick and Teddington, and in 1965 the Borough was in turn united with Richmond and Barnes to form the London Borough of Richmond upon Thames. York House continued to be the centre of civic affairs for the new borough, but the opening of the new Civic Centre in York Street in 1990 has provided an opportunity for some of its rooms to be restored to their former state when it was a private house.

The libraries of the area have been brought into one system in two stages, in 1937 and in 1965, and are now administered from Richmond.

143. *A 'bed-poster' fire engine, of the sort once possessed by Twickenham's fire brigade, in action (see over).*

144.   Twickenham Fire Brigade outside the Fire Station in Queen's Road, pre 1915.

TWICKENHAM'S FIREFIGHTERS

Fire has always been a good servant but a bad master, and as communities developed its potential destructiveness grew more serious. After the Great Fire of London in 1666 insurance companies were established and in order to minimise losses set up their own fire brigades. Fire insurance marks on buildings indicated which company's interests were involved. Outside London these marks still served to encourage potential helpers, and there are several still to be seen in Twickenham, particularly in Montpelier Row.

Insurance companies encouraged the establishment of local fire brigades in areas where their own did not operate. It is perhaps due to the initiative of the Westminster Insurance Company (four of whose signs survive in Montpelier Row), which contributed £5.5.0d to the subscription list, that Twickenham owes its first engine in 1738. Whatever its origin, the subscription list in the churchwardens' accounts totals £85.3.6d. Expenses of engines with three dozen leather buckets (£84.4.0d) and sundry expenses totalled £87.14.10d, the balance being paid from parish funds. The Duke of Somerset allocated space near the churchyard for an engine house. It is probable that the large engine was of the type known as a 'bedposter', with a pump driven by a pivoted bar oper-

ated by several men. In 1785 rules for the maintenance and use of the engines were adopted, and four local employers of labour assigned three men each to form a team to work the engines, six being available at any one time. They were paid, generously by the then current value of money, 2/6d for bringing the engines and a shilling an hour when working them. The engines were later housed in Back Lane (now Holly Road). New regulations were drawn up in 1834 though there is a certain lack or urgency in the arrangement whereby the men concerned should collect their badges before going to the fire.

The Local Board of Health established in 1868 soon decided to set up a Fire Brigade, with a volunteer force consisting of Captain John Bowyer (corn chandler), Engineer George Davis (plumber) and eight others, all of them local tradesmen. An engine-keeper was paid 2s 6d per week. At first a steam pump engine was hired, but in 1870 it was decided to purchase one at a cost of £348. The Duc d'Aumale contributed 100 guineas towards this, and the engine was named Orleans in his honour. In 1875 it was given a permanent home in a new fire station in Queen's Road, next to the Local Board offices.

The Brigade not only fought fires, but had an active social life, with suppers, excursions, and the organisation of a cricket team. However, in 1891 it was decided to place the Brigade under a professional officer, Henry Day, who had been appointed superintendent. Day died a few months later and John 'Jock' Cameron then took over and remained in command during a period of considerable development which included the formation of a fully-paid brigade.

A volunteer brigade was reformed during the 1st World War when most of the firemen joined the forces. Jock Cameron, then about 76, came out of retirement to go on duty and he still continued to drop in until he died at the age of 93 in 1931. Gradually after the war the brigade returned to being a professional force and the formal end of the volunteers was recognised in 1923 when the Urban District Council issued silver medals to its members. The new brigade was under the command of William Woods who, having joined it at the age of 18 in 1899, retired as its Chief Officer in 1941.

CARING FOR THE SICK AND POOR

Under the Poor Law Act of 1601 churchwardens were made responsible for the care of the parish poor, though there were Overseers of the Poor to carry out the main duties. The parish records of Twickenham show that initially the usual method was by outdoor relief, paid for by a poor rate and by various charitable donations.

In 1703 six almshouses were built on the north side of the Common from a legacy of Mathew Harvie, and six more added in 1721. Four years later, following the Workhouse Test Act of 1722, a workhouse was built adjoining them. This proximity had its problems. In 1735 three occupants of the almshouses were expelled for selling spirits to the workhouse, and later the workhouse took over some of the almshouse premises. There were other difficulties - the dismissal of an unsatisfactory Master, disputes with suppliers of food, and presumably disciplinary troubles, since the erection of a whipping post was ordered in 1790. A pleasanter aspect was shown in the regulations of 1788, when it was ordered that at Easter, Whitsun and Christmas the inmates ' shall be accommodated with Plumb Puddings.' Following the Poor Law Amendment Act of 1834 the Brentford Union was created to meet the needs of a group of neighbouring towns. A large workhouse was built in the grounds of the present-day West Middlesex Hospital, and the Twickenham building was sold - by the mid-1840s it had been demolished.

A rather different approach to problems of poverty was that of the Rev. G.S. Master, vicar of Twickenham 1859-1865. He founded a variety of thrift schemes, including the Twickenham Penny Bank, the Boot and Shoe Club, and the Clothing and Fuel Club, all based

145. *Elizabeth Twining*

on the principle of encouraging small savers by adding tangible interest to their deposits; these institutions continued in changing circumstances well into the next century.

In the 1820s it was decided to create new almshouses in School Alley, near St Mary's church; these were rebuilt on a slightly different site in 1876 at the expense of Miss Elizabeth Twining of Dial House. William Candler left a bequest for new almshouses on his death in 1907, but it was not until 1935 that the Twickenham Charities were consolidated and the following year new almshouses, including those provided for by Candler's legacy, were opened in Amyand Park Road. Ten almshouses provided by the Carpenters' Company were built in the Hampton Road in 1841-2 but in 1947 the site was sold to Twickenham Council for £5,000 and the building demolished: the site is marked by a block of flats, begun in 1950, called Carpenters' Court.

There are scattered early references to illness in Twickenham, particularly among the poor. The Church registers record the customary large infant mortality, and list deaths from plague in 1603 and 1665. A court case of 1640 concerned a dog which had been allowed into the pest house and thus might

146. St John's Hospital; an early engraving.

147. Patients in the garden of St John's Hospital c1908.

have spread infection. An apothecary to attend to the needs of the poor was appointed in 1780.

Twickenham's hospital was founded by Elizabeth Twining in 1879, to be known as the Twining Hospital and, at her request, dedicated to St John the Baptist. It was opened in 1880, but soon closed owing to financial and administrative problems. In 1885 it was reopened with Vincent Griffiths as chairman of its committee, a post he was to occupy with distinction for many years. Extensions were opened by the Princess Royal in 1932 and a generous gift from the Cartwright Trust in 1974 made possible further additions. It served as a cottage hospital for the area, as well as containing X-ray and other auxiliary services, though the West Middlesex Hospital was increasingly used for more serious cases. St John's Hospital was finally closed in 1988 and suffered much from vandalism, but is now in course of rebuilding as a psychogeriatric hospital.

The Local Board set up an isolation hospital at the Mereway in 1883; in 1909 a 'fever hospital' to replace it was opened in Nelson Road. This was closed when Twickenham combined with Richmond, Heston and Isleworth to open a new isolation hospital in Mogden Lane (later known as the South Middlesex Hospital) in 1937.

Mention may also be made of the private asylum run by Dr Hugh Welch Diamond at Twickenham House in Heath Road from 1858 until his death in 1887. Diamond was also a pioneer photographer, particularly in his faithful if sometimes gruesome recording of the appearance of his patients.

NEWSPAPERS

In 1854 the *Surrey Comet* of Kingston was founded, and from time to time included Twickenham news, but the first local paper to concentrate on the locality was *The Richmond and Twickenham Times; a Journal of Local News, Society, and Literature, for Richmond, Twickenham, Teddington, Petersham, Mortlake, Kew, Ham, &c.* It was founded by Edward King of Richmond, and first appeared on 31 May 1873. Its first leader declared ' In political matters we take an INDEPENDENT position, as we cannot believe in an infallible party on either side of the House...In our reports of local matters, we shall endeavour to combine variety with brevity...' A major feature of the Twickenham news, as it continued to be for some time, was the problem of drainage and sewage.

Frederick W. Dimbleby, who joined the staff in 1874, purchased the paper when King retired in 1894 and it is still owned by the family, the central publication of a group of local newspapers. For many years there was a mid-week edition, *The Thames Valley Times*, but this is no longer published.

148. Prospectus of The Richmond and Twickenham Times, *31 May 1873.*

149. *Gas Board office in March Road. Photograph by Alan Urwin.*

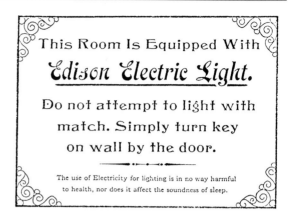

150. *Electric light notice New York 1882, similar to those used in England.*

LIGHTING UP THE TOWN

Until the 19th century, as elsewhere in England, Twickenham mainly depended on oil lamps, rushes and torches dipped in resin or beeswax, and tallow candles. In 1681 oil lamps began to be used in London, and in 1784 the Argand oil lamp with a tubular wick and with a much stronger light, was introduced. Gas light was first used in 1795 to light a house, but gas did not reach Twickenham until 1858, and then only by pipeline from Brentford. Electricity was first used for lighting in 1812 but this was not possible on an industrial scale until 1831 when Faraday showed that it could be produced by electromagnetic induction and generated by mechanical means, and after 1871 when the dynamo appeared.

In Twickenham the Local Board first had a Lighting Committee in 1868, but this was mainly involved in complaints, suggestions and negotiations with the Brentford Gas Company. It did not consider electricity until 1882, and in that year too it was approached by the West Middlesex Electric Lights Company for permission to 'lay their wires in the Parish', but no interest was aroused. Three other companies made approaches in 1888 without any success. By 1892 the Local Board became more positive and considered 'whether any other way can be suggested for lighting the Parish or any part thereof'. The Gas Lobby was in danger!

Advice was now taken. The roads from Richmond Bridge to Strawberry Vale were then mainly lit by 155 ordinary street gas lamps at a cost of £580, but the provision of electricity for street lighting would require an income of £5,000 per annum from private consumers. The expense and the decision was too much for the Lighting Committee and electricity slipped off the agenda and all was quiet until 1898. In that year Edmunson's Electricity Corporation offered to form a local supply company, and H. Jason Saunders, the Clerk to the Council, was authorised to enquire into the situation in other towns and dis-

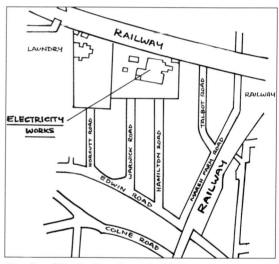

151. *Site of Twickenham Electricity Works 1915.*

tricts. He reported that 'the Engineers are mostly agreed that Electricity is not cheaper than gas...' and that local authorities only introduced it to improve street lighting and not for cheapness.

Co-operation with neighbouring councils was then considered. Richmond Electric Light and Power Company, formed in 1893, offered to provide current within months from the Richmond Generating Station, whereas a new station would take two years to build in Twickenham. Still no decision was taken.

Eventually, in July 1900, consent was approved for Edmunson's and the Twickenham and Teddington Electric Supply Company to supply electricity, and the buildings for a power station in Edwin Road were begun in 1901. The supply was initiated on 21 July 1902.

A PLACE OF LEARNING

The earliest reference to a school in Twickenham occurs in the records of St Mary's church in the 1640s, with a mention of a schoolmaster and the need for repairs to the house where he was 'keeping school'. The house was close to the Embankment and the master had the use of one or more rooms rent free. Shortly afterwards a girls' (or maids') department was begun, possibly in a separate building. In 1669 the school closed or moved elsewhere, but in 1682 efforts were made to evict the occupant of the house so that the school might be restarted. It was 1686, however, before a William Lawrence was appointed a master, and the start of the 18th century saw an altogether new development.

In 1704 the Society for Promoting Christian Knowledge (founded in 1699) opened a charity school in 'Twittenham' which built on the earlier parochial initiative. Fifty pupils were clothed and educated by voluntary contributions; between twenty and thirty boys were taught to read and write, and the girls, being intended for 'common servants', were taught to read only. Much of the reading material consisted of the Catechism and *Book of Common Prayer*, and for part of the day the pupils were set to menial trade work. There was enlarged scope for some with the setting up in the 1720s of the West Charity which provided for poor children from Reading, Twickenham and Newbury to be endowed at Christ's Hospital in the City, a provision which exists till this day. In 1747 the boys' school moved to a house in Twickenham's 'East End', but in 1773, when this house was said to be in danger of collapsing, the school was moved to Bell Lane (or Crazy Lane as it was then known). Such schools were never popular with poorer parents, since while their children were at school they lost a potential source of income. Thus Sunday Schools tended to be more acceptable, following their inauguration in the 1780s.

In the late 18th and early 19th centuries private schools began to appear in this fashionable riverside district. The Rev. L.M. Stretch's Academy was in London Road from 1782 to 1788; Mrs Pomeroy's Female Boarding School in the same road was opposite Grosvenor House, and Miss Dutton's Female Boarding School, at the junction of the London and Amyand Park Roads, is said to have had Mary

152. Schoolchildren walking in East Twickenham; detail from engraving of c1817

Wollstonecraft Godwin as a pupil. A National School was set up in 1809, housed in premises on the east side of School Alley, which ran from Church Street to the Embankment, parallel with D'Aumale Cottages and Church Lane. This school had 180 pupils and was organised on Dr Bell's 'Madras' system. A large room was marked into squares, in which children stood to say their lessons, whilst writing desks were ranged against the walls. One master presided with the aid of an assistant teacher (aged between 11 and 14) and other 'monitors' or 'tutors' aged from 7 to 11. It was thought to be the cheapest way to mass-produce learning.

At the time the railway arrived in 1848 the town was expanding westwards and so it was around the Green that the next developments occurred. In 1834 a British School had been established, next to the Independent (now URC) chapel on the Hampton Road and First Cross Road corner, but the opening of the Trafalgar school in 1904 caused this to decline sharply and to fade out of existence at the start of the 1st World War. In 1841 Holy Trinity church was consecrated and in the following years its Archdeacon Cambridge school was opened in Vicarage Road. The Montpelier School, opened in Orleans Road in 1856, and from 1863 St Mary's parochial school moved from School Alley to its present site on the Arragon/Amyand Park Road corner.

In Whitton an elementary school was founded in 1851 in the grounds of Kneller Hall while the house was occupied by the short-lived government training college for teachers of pauper and delinquent children.

By 1870 the three National or parochial schools and the British School accommodated some 1,000 pupils out of a potential of about 2,500. A Society of Arts report of 1870 found that the expense per head on education in affluent Twickenham was 'lower than in any surrounding parish.' No Board Schools were set up in Twickenham after Forster's 1870 Elementary Education Act because residents were persuaded that they would be more expensive than parochial schools. Ratepayers were under constant threat, and ludicrously obsessive dread, of the introduction of a School Board right to the end of the century. The year 1893, however, did see the opening of St James's Roman Catholic School in Grosvenor Road.

Under the Balfour Education Act of 1902 urban districts such as Twickenham, with a population of 20,000, became authorities for the elementary education in their area. The first meeting of the formally constituted Education Committee for Twickenham took place in June 1903. School managers were appointed, a new school (Trafalgar) was opened in Third Cross Road in 1904, and the Orleans School off Richmond Road followed in 1910. In Whitton the Nelson Road School was opened in 1911.

153. *Children of Trafalgar School assembled in the playground 1912.*

154. *Children round a maypole at Whitton Church of England School, Kneller Road, c1912.*

As for secondary education, the Twickenham County School for Girls was opened in Clifden Road in 1909, and in the following year arrangements were made for about a third of the pupils at Hampton Grammar School to come from Twickenham.

The Fisher Education Act of 1918 raised the school-leaving age to fourteen. More schools were opened between the wars. The Thames Valley School for Boys and Girls (1928), the Kneller School in Meadway (1936), and the Twickenham Technical College and School of Art (1937); in 1977 this became the site of the Richmond upon Thames Tertiary College for 16-19-year-olds.

155. *Part of an Inspector's Report on Montpelier Female School, 1864, from its log book.*

badly taught.
Two tenths have been deducted from the grant earned under Article 40 (Revised Code) on account of the very defective instruction (Art 52(a)).
I am to request your attention to the ninth Supplementary Rule
A Log book (articles 55(a) and 56—63) and Portfolio (article 55(b) must be provided
The School accounts must in future be submitted to H.M's Inspector and should be duly Audited
The Mistress is warned that she must receive better certificates from the managers next year and my lords decline to issue her certificate until a better report has been received from H.M's Inspector.
(Grimman*

On Wheels and Waves

Twickenham lies trapped in a great bend of the Thames and the old Roman road through Staines passed it by. Until the 18th century the local roads were little more than dirt tracks; heavy goods came by way of the river and up until the early 19th century a crane stood at the water's edge at the end of Wharf Lane. Generally people travelled by horse, by donkey, or by foot. A few had their private carriages: in 1744 Mr Glass's 'chariot' killed James Smith, aged eight years, in Twickenham (the carriage was adjudged a 'deodand' an item that could be confiscated as being 'responsible' for causing a death).

Local travel began to improve in the 18th century with the introduction of turnpike roads - the Isleworth, Twickenham and Teddington turnpike of the late 1760s, and then that of Hampton to Staines in the 1770s. In this last decade the first local bridge across the Thames was opened, in 1777, linking Richmond to Twickenham. Previously passengers had depended on various ferries including the horse ferry to Richmond that had taken carriages across.

Stage coaches developed as an important means of communication; by 1833 eight were passing daily through Twickenham, and horses were changed at two inns in King Street: outward traffic at the George and inward at the King's Head.

Richmond Bridge was financed by a 'tontine' and tolls were charged until 1859. Before that date, however, the next great transport revolution had brought the railway to Twickenham in 1848, with additional stations being added at Strawberry Hill in 1873 (on the loopline to Kingston, built in 1863) and at St Margaret's in 1876. The inhabitants of Whitton village had to depend on the Hounslow station (then called 'Hounslow and Whitton') until the new Whitton station was opened in July 1930.

The railway was not universally popular, particularly in its early days and the local press carried protests about the lack of safety at level crossings,

156. Richmond Railway Bridge from the Surrey bank.

particularly after an elderly lady was killed on one in 1866, and there were also complaints about the 'horrid clangour' of the station bell announcing the imminent arrival of a train.

The commercial use of the river declined as railways developed and road transport - at first horse-drawn, and after the turn of the century mechanical - flourished along improved roads. There were other problems connected with the river. A local headmaster complained of the lawlessness of the waterside boys and watermen's helpers who tended to drunkenness and the chalking of vulgar words on walls. During the summer they enjoyed good wages and 'affect high style and have their champagne fights'; whilst for their numerous regatta days they sought subscriptions from the gentry and the tradesmen for the purposes of drink.

Steam had, of course, come to the river even earlier, shortly after the Battle of Waterloo. But steamers had only a limited success, subject to the snags and hazards of the river as they were, and were used mainly by day trippers.

The transport revolution was reflected in the sevenfold increase of Twickenham's population between 1801 and 1901. Trams were introduced into Twickenham in 1903 and buses in 1910. The first trolleybuses in the London area ran from Fulwell depot to Twickenham Junction, and thence to Teddington, from May 1931; these gradually replaced the trams, but were themselves displaced by diesel buses, and the last one ran in 1962.

To cope with the increase of traffic Richmond Bridge was widened between 1937 and 1939, and early in that decade the Chertsey Road by-pass was completed and the link to the Surrey bank completed with the opening of Twickenham Bridge in 1933. Earlier still the problems of the river began to be addressed by the construction of the Richmond half lock, opened in 1894. This lock also provided a crossing for foot passengers for a toll of a penny a person.

157. *Pleasure steamer* Diamond *off Eel Pie Island c1850.*

158. *Cabs waiting outside Twickenham railway station.*

159. *An early tram by Holy Trinity church, Twickenham Green.*

Working Lives

Glover's map of Twickenham in 1635 shows 'Coole's Brewery' on the London Road near the site of the present Regal House. This brewery, the first evidence of industry in Twickenham, later moved across the road where it remained in the possession of the Cole family until the late 19th century, and was still in operation in 1927. There were two other major breweries in the parish. One was in London Road on the north side of the present York Street in the 19th century, and another behind the Red Lion in Heath Road.

THE GUNPOWDER MILLS

Glover's map shows a windmill in Whitton at the edge of the heath, east of the junction of the present Percy and Hospital Bridge Roads. After the Duke of Northumberland's River had been built in the 1540s the reinforced stretch of the Crane, between Feltham and Twickenham, was the site of two mills. The first was near Fulwell, which may have been a copper mill for a time but by 1767 was being used to make linseed oil and cattle cake; between 1845 and 1865 it

made paper, and then it was burnt down and not rebuilt. The second mill was possibly on the site of a medieval mill. It was opened as a corn mill around 1757 but was manufacturing gunpowder by 1766. Edmund Hill, the first owner, is reputed to have made nearly a million pounds from his ownership. Explosions causing deaths and injuries were reported frequently through the 18th and 19th centuries. Some of them annoyed Walpole at Strawberry Hill when his windows were broken.

Throughout the 19th century the mills were owned by the company of Curtis and Harvey, who had bought them in 1820. In 1850 the works were described thus:

'The buildings are nearly all placed at some distance from each other, and those where the more dangerous processes of manufacture are carried on, are carefully secluded from the rest by thick belts of firewood, by mounds of earth, or by such other means as the positions in which they are placed. Nearly all the buildings are constructed of the lightest material so they would offer the least resistance to an explosion.'

In their heyday in 1859 the mills employed 320 men and women, and although there were a number of fatalities from the explosions there was a queue to

160. Aftermath of explosion in gunpowder mills 1859.

G. and E. POWELL,

Opposite the OLD CHURCH,

TWICKENHAM.

SILK MERCERS, DRAPERS, HOSIERS

AND

HABERDASHERS.

Family Linen, Carpet, and Bedding Warehouse.

ESTABLISHED 80 YEARS.

Gentlemen Furnishing will find an Excellent Assortment of BRUSSELS, TAPESTRY, and other CARPETS, of the Newest Styles, and at London Prices.

Blinds of all kinds Made and Fixed; Estimates given if desired.

UNDERTAKERS.

Agents to the Sun Fire and Life Offices.

161. Advertisement for Powell's the drapers in Church Street.

162. Corben Brothers Carriage Repository, Heath Road, from Phillipson's Kingston Directory 1893.

work there. The Hounslow Mills at the end of the 19th century were making high-class powder for military and sporting purposes and had succeeded in establishing a worldwide reputation; they were an important part of the war effort from 1914 to 1918.

Curtis and Harvey were taken over by Nobel Industries in 1920, which themselves were absorbed into the merger which formed ICI. The decision was then taken to move the manufacture of gunpowder from Hounslow as the area was then in the process of urban development; the closure of Hounslow works occurred in 1927.

The site was sold, partly for housing and that part along the banks of the Crane was acquired by Twickenham Council and landscaped as a public park.

OTHER VENTURES

The Corben family opened their carriage factory in Richmond Road, on the corner of Oak Lane, in 1852. This became a motor works in the present century and is now a Volvo garage. Another carriage manufacturer in Twickenham was James Hargreaves Mann, whose advertisement claimed he was 'By appointment to Her Majesty, the Prince of Wales, and Princes of the Orleans Family'.

Commercial fish hatcheries in the river Crane and lamprey fisheries in the Thames were begun in the 19th century.

Twickenham Film Studios at St Margaret's opened in 1913: its productions range from an early version of *Bulldog Drummond* to the Beatles' *Hard Day's Night* and Richard Attenborough's *Gandhi*.

163. C.F. Latter's hardware store at 32 Staines Road, at the beginning of the 20th century.

164. *Bowyer's Wharf, Twickenham. Built in 1897 for the Bowyer family, corn and coal merchants, it was much criticised for impeding the view of St Mary's church from the river. It was demolished in 1960.*

THE MARKET GARDENS

Twickenham has been home to some notable gardeners, nurseymen and horticulturists. Earliest was Francis Bacon, the first Englishman to concern himself as a scientist with agriculture, and whose observations and experiments were published in *Sylva Sylvarium*. The area has seen the whole range of gardens from those typical of medieval agricultural economy to those fashioned by gentlemen and nobility in the 17th and 18th centuries. There were also the grounds of nurserymen and commercial market gardeners: Twickenham and Isleworth were the main constituents of the then garden of England before strawberries moved to Kent, houses replaced the raspberries and the 'cabbage patch' became the home of Rugby football.

Notable early Twickenham gardens were those of Vincent Pointer (or Corbet) who lived here from 1590 to 1616, 'a most cunning grafter and planter of all manner of rare fruits', and of Mr Craston, who had several enclosed nurseries and orchards just east of the church, the manor house and the grounds of the later Orleans House.

Daniel Langley, father of the more famous Batty, undertook work at Twickenham Park just after 1700, and Alexander Pope's gardener, John Searle, left us

a plan of Pope's riverside garden and the five acres reached via his grotto. At Whitton the Duke of Argyll was noted for his cultivation of exotic trees and plants, but all these were private and not commercial gardens.

In 1797 Edward Ironside observed that 'The parts round Twickenham are greatly distinguished by the fertility of its well-cultivated garden grounds, which send large supplies of vegetables and fruits, particularly strawberries, to the London markets. The more open enclosures furnish great quantities of early peas. Mr Nettleship, a very intelligent and skilful gardener, annually produces a great variety of the finest early flowers, as well as early fruits, by well contrived and extensive stoves.'

The profitability of market gardening and fruit farming increased the demand for manure and drove prices upwards. At one time the City had had to pay for street cleaning, but by 1800 money was paid for the privilege. In 1763 stable dung sold for three pence a load, but by 1793 it had risen to two shillings a load. Horticulture and the intensive cultivation that was undertaken could never have come about without the natural manures available from London. Twickenham, Isleworth and Hounslow also had the benefit of manure from the post and coaching inns on the Bath Road and, after 1793, the barracks at Hounslow.

Hot houses and greenhouses were widely used, as also was the shadoof, an irrigation device consisting of a pole with a bucket and counterweight, originating in Egypt, as there was a regular water supply at eight to ten feet below ground.

In 1848 there were 184 acres of market garden, mostly in the north and north east of the town, moving later in the century towards Whitton as building took place in the land north of Twickenham centre.

In the 1880s William Poupart developed a market garden on Marsh Farm, now a Council depot, which concentrated on apples, pears, plums and cherries and in 1911 a jam factory using produce from these fields was opened in Third Cross Road by the Poupart family.

Some growers specialised in flowers and one was sufficiently known for his orchid cultivation to be subject of an article in the *Gardener's World* magazine in 1889: 'The houses at the Amyand Park Road branch nursery of Mr. W. Gordon, Twickenham, are entirely devoted to the cultivation of Orchids.'

The 1894 25-inch Ordnance Survey shows the extent of the nurseries between Twickenham and Richmond, St Margaret's Road and the railway. Mr Gordon's orchid nursery is clearly indicated by a number of greenhouses. All the open nursery, garden and orchard lands shown on this map are now covered by turn-of-the-century houses and mainly 1930s semi-detached maisonettes and flats.

167. William Bates' Nursery shown on the 1914 Ordnance Survey map.

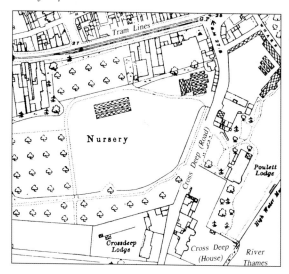

165. Shadoof used in local market gardening

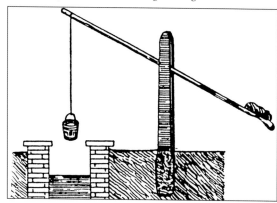

166. Nurseries and orchards in East Twickenham from the 1894 Ordnance Survey map.

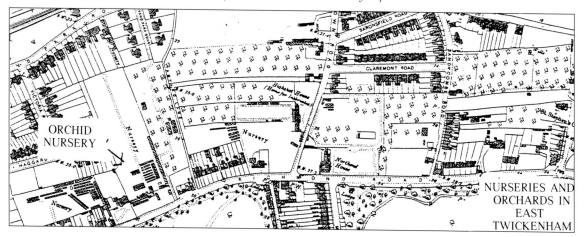

The largest market garden, however, was begun in 1891 when William Whiteley, the 'Universal Provider' and the owner of Whiteley's store in Westbourne Grove, purchased nearly 200 acres on the borders of Twickenham and Hounslow. In the next five years he converted this into an industrial enterprise, growing fruit and vegetables, rearing pigs, cows, bees, dogs, wild and tame rabbits and making fruit preserves, potted meats, soups, squashes, confectionery, invalid specialities, pickles, sauces and table delicacies. The estate was surrounded by a 6-feet high galvanised iron wall planted outside with privet and hawthorn.

The grounds contained an astonishing number of plants and trees. There were, for example, nearly 35,000 blackcurrant trees, 284,000 raspberry trees, 881,000 strawberry plants, 14,217 apple trees etc.

Unfortunately, the project was never completely viable and was short-lived.

Probably the last commercial garden in central Twickenham was the Cross Deep Nursery. It probably derived from the kitchen garden of Poulett Lodge across the road on the riverside, and is today represented by Poulett Gardens. About 1875 it was operated as a garden by William Bates, who had come to Twickenham from Staffordshire. About half of the main nursery consisted of fruit trees (plums, peaches, cherries etc), and on the open ground were mushrooms, loganberries, strawberries etc and always flowers.

In the 19th century Whitton was noted for roses, narcissi and lilies of the valley, and also for apples, plums and pears. Piggeries were also prominent but these disappeared as building extended there in the 1920s.

168. *Poupart's Jam Factory, Twickenham.*

Leisurely Days

GLIDING ON THE RIVER

As we have seen (p79) a bowling alley is shown on Eel Pie Island on Glover's map of 1635. This would have been a game more like the French *boule* than the present English green bowling. Perhaps local resident, the poet Sir John Suckling, known for his enthusiasm for the game, played here. In recent years, bowling has become a very popular local amateur sport.

Many engravings of Twickenham from the Thames show rowing boats on the river, and though most of these were engaged in commercial activities, rowing as a sport has a long tradition. The scandalous diarist, William Hickey, whose father Joseph was a respected local resident, records many episodes of sailing and rowing, beginning in his boyhood, and in 1765 was wont to row at weekends from London to his parents' summer residence at Twickenham, a distance of some eighteen miles.

Twickenham Rowing Club was founded in 1860, with the Treasury official, Vincent Griffiths, a well-known local resident, as Secretary and the Duc d'Aumale as President. It was active in social and dramatic activities as well as in rowing, and in 1865 the Irish composer, Vincent Wallace, wrote *The Oarsman's March*, dedicated to its members. In 1880 its boathouse and clubhouse on Eel Pie Island was constructed. By this time the Club's rowing prowess had improved greatly due to the skills of Leonard Frere, a highly successful stroke, and the Cambridge oarsman, John Goldie. The club still exists.

Competitive rowing found an outlet in various regattas in Twickenham and neighbouring towns - Horace Walpole wrote of a local boat race at Richmond in 1791. For many years the Boys and Girls' Regatta, founded by Twickenham waterman, Charlie Shore, was a much enjoyed popular annual event for its sideshows, contests such as the greasy pole, and fireworks, as well as for its rowing, and the Twickenham Amateur Regatta was founded in 1923. Recreational rowing on the river was very popular between the wars.

A noted oarsman who lived in Twickenham for more than half a century until his death, aged 94, in 1968 was Ernest Barry, who won Doggett's Coat and Badge in 1903, became a Royal Waterman ten years later, and was five times Champion World Sculler between 1912 and 1920.

169. Twickenham Boys and Girls' Regatta, c1910

170. *A group of Twickenham Rowing Club. Vincent Griffiths is the bearded figure on the right. It is believed that the Rev. R.S. Cobbett is in this group.*

171. *Dr. W.G. Grace in the centre of a group taken on the occasion of a match on Twickenham Green between W.Strutt-Cavell's XII v XVIII of Twickenham, 19 September 1905, which raised £80 for the funds of St John's Hospital.*

EARLY CRICKET

Lord John Sackville, who preceded Walpole at Strawberry Hill, initiated some local cricket. William Hickey had some reputation as a wicket-keeper, and Laetitia Hawkins recalled being a 'supernumary scout' in games on the lawn of Gifford Lodge in the 1760s. The 19th century saw the development of organised sport. The Twickenham Cricket Club was formed in 1833; its early matches were probably played in a field off the Hampton Road belonging to William Withers, a butcher, who was its first Secretary, but later the venue was Twickenham Green. The first recorded match, which Twickenham won by six wickets, was against Thames Ditton, and the two teams met for a centenary match on the Green in 1933; this event was also marked by a period costume match. Probably the most distinguished visiting play-

ers at Twickenham were Dr W.G. Grace, who played in charity matches on the Green, and the Australian 'demon bowler', F.H. Spofforth, who appeared at the Orleans Club in 1878. An unusual match was played in 1884 on the bed of the river Thames made possible by the effects of a very dry spring and summer.

Twickenham was also associated with skating after the Sports-Drome opened in 1928 in part of the former Pelabon munitions works in East Twickenham. Redesigned in the 1930s, the ice-rink which was its main feature was a venue for international contests and the training of notable skaters, as well as a popular local centre for family recreation. It was closed in January 1992 and demolished for housing development.

172. *Cricket played on the bed of the Thames, 21 June 1884, and other activities made possible by drought.*

THE RUGBY GROUND - 'BILLY WILLIAMS' CABBAGE PATCH'

Twickenham is known world-wide as the home of English rugby. That this came about was due entirely to one man, Billy Williams. He was a fine all-round sportsman, playing first-class cricket for Middlesex (he wasplaying at club level at the age of 74, when he was still taking a hundred wickets in a season). He played rugby for Harlequins, later became a first-class referee, and was also regularly playing golf till his death at the age of 90 in 1951. In the early 1900s the Rugby Football Union was looking for a site to develop as a home ground for England matches and also as a headquarters. It was Billy Williams, then a member of the Middlesex Committee, who found an area of ten acres off the Whitton Road, then in use as a market garden. The land was bought by the Union in 1907 and in October 1909 the ground was opened for its first match, Harlequins *v* Richmond. The first England international there, against Wales, took place the following January. In the early years the ground acquired the name 'Billy Williams' Cabbage Patch' as an affectionate reminder of its origins.

Initially the ground held some 30,000 spectators,

173. *Aerial photograph of the Rugby Ground in 1927, with the surrounding area still largely unbuilt.*

with 6,000 seated in the single tiered east and west stands. After the 1st World War the capacity was increased by having a double-decker east stand and building a new north stand, so that in 1925 60,000 people saw the clash with the unbeaten All Blacks. In 1932 a new double-decker west stand was built, bringing the capacity up to 73,000, a number which saw Prince Obolensky's famous try against the third All Blacks.

174. *Poster for the Rugby Ground, 1921, by Dame Laura Knight.*

ANGLING

Anglers often appear in the foreground of engravings of Twickenham, and it was clearly a popular riverside sport. Sir John Hawkins, who lived at Twickenham House in the 1760s, edited Walton's *Compleat Angler*, and prided himself on throwing a line fourteen yards long, baited with a fly of his own making.

Changes in the sport have come since. The gradual inflow of the tides has moved the meeting point of salt and fresh water upstream, and there has been much pollution both from the building of the gasworks by the river after 1807 and the increase in local population. There has also been a reduction in the volume of the water caused not only by extraction above Teddington to serve London after 1855, but by the increased flow of water downstream due to improved bridges and embankments. By 1866 these last two factors had reduced the water level at Richmond Bridge by 3ft 6ins.

The Thames Angling Preservation Society, founded at the Bell at Hampton in 1838, was a response to concern about the river. To add to regulations as to the size of fish that might be caught, netting was abolished between Twickenham and Staines, and the Thames Conservancy was persuaded to upgrade its bye-laws. Several 'deeps' or preserved fishing waters were also secured, including 700 yards from just below Richmond Bridge to the Three Pigeons on the Richmond bank, and 400 yards above the site of Pope's Villa. Regular reports in the *Richmond & Twickenham Times* from 1873, giving conditions and catches during the season also helped. At this time dace, barbel, roach, chub, gudgeon and jack were regularly caught and trout up to ten and even seventeen pounds above the tidal waters. But stocks continued to decline and in 1865 Francis Francis (1822-86), who lived in The Firs in the Staines Road (he was fishing editor of *The Field* for 25 years and a nationally famous angler) reported:

'Formerly the Thames was perhaps one of the most productive rivers in the kingdom. But poaching, over-fishing, unfair and unsportsmanlike fishing, its conversion into a sewer and into a canal, the abstraction of a very large quantity of its water by Water Companies, and the super-abundance of swans, which a mistaken and extravagant appetite for the picturesque has crowded it with, have all contrib-

175. Francis Francis fishing in the River Crane, from the watercolour by A.W. Cooper.

176. *Fish rearing house at Twickenham.*

uted to render fishing on it for a very considerable portion of the year, and, save under very favourable circumstances, a very bootless occupation.'

An investigation in 1957/8 by the London Natural History Society concluded that there was no evidence of fish life in the Thames between Chiswick and Greenwich. Since then, thankfully, the situation has been brought under control and the river restocked. The success with salmon, which was extinct in the river by 1820, has received the greatest publicity - a dead salmon, found in August 1990 by Richmond Bridge, and evidently killed by a boat propeller, was almost a metre in length.

FISH REARING AT THE FIRS

The Francis Francis mentioned above made an important contribution to fishing. In the early 1860s he built a fish rearing house by his house, The Firs,

which had grounds backing on to the river Crane. In 1864 the *Illustrated London News* showed the interior of this and gave a detailed description of the workings of the rearing system. He also helped to organise a similar venture at Hampton for the Thames Angling Preservation Society, and from here between 1861 and 1866, 4,800 salmon, 4,000 sea trout, 137,000 trout and some char and grayling were released into the Thames. But the enterprise travelled further than the Thames. In January 1864 a consignment of around 100,000 salmon ova and some 3,000 trout were delivered to London Docks and packed in moss and ice was sent to Tasmania. Of the salmon only 3,000 were hatched but these died in the cooler sea water, but 171 trout fry did survive to be released into Tasmanian rivers and from these came the present-day magnificent trout of New Zealand, Australia and Tasmania.

Suburbia to the Nth Degree

In the 20th century Twickenham and Whitton can be said to have topped out. Population peaked at nearly 53,000 in 1951 and thirty years later was down by 12,000. Certainly by 1950 there were no pieces of land of significant size left for housing development, and only very occasional infilling can now be seen. Generally the houses built in this century have been semi-detached, particularly in the extremities of Whitton to the north, Strawberry Hill to the south, East Twickenham and the old Powder Mills area to the west.

GROUND LEVELS

The only high points in Twickenham are those where the village was first established in the region of St Mary's church - the slope of roads leading up from the river is quite noticeable. Present day develop-

ment disguises the old ground levels. Before, say, 1850 there were remains of gravel and sand pits, and there were clay pits for brickmaking. In Twickenham Park and at Gordon House mounds were a garden feature, and some are still there; in 1722 Batty Langley converted a sand pit, 'a nuisance', into a spiral garden with bushes and trees, perhaps 100 feet in diameter, 'a very agreeable beautiful figure as it now appears...'. There was also a gravel pit in the area of Ellesmere Road where one or two 1930s houses have had foundation problems in recent years, and Park House Gardens was a gravel pit up to the 1930s. Marble Hill was terraced towards the river, probably in Lady Suffolk's time, and the level cricket pitch at the main road side dates from the laying out as a sports ground. The lower original ground level and the undulating nature of the land at one time can be seen behind J.M.W. Turner's house in Sandycombe Road, and behind the house and yard of Eldridge & Son, builders and decorators, at the corner of Sandycombe and St Margaret's Roads, looking just as it did at the turn of this century. In the 1920s the site and grounds of Orleans House were excavated for gravel.

177. Church Street 1900; lithograph by T.R. Way.

178. King Street, 1900; lithograph by T.R. Way

179. Saluting the Flag on Twickenham Green on George V's Coronation Day, 18 June 1911.

180. *Aerial view of Twickenham Bridge under construction 1932, showing the railway bridge near it. The Elms is seen to the right of the bridge.*

181. *Late 19th-century semi-detached house, with one entrance in Rosslyn Road and another in Arlington Road, Twickenham Park. Photograph by Alan Urwin.*

THE END OF TWICKENHAM PARK

Building on the grounds of the larger remaining mansions still continued in the 20th century. The last major development introduced Beresford Avenue and Park House Gardens in the 1930s.

The land that became Beresford Avenue had always been open. Possibly in medieval times it had been part of the rabbit warren, included in the Park and used for hunting or keeping deer. During the time of the Duchess of Newcastle it had been cultivated as farm or meadow land, but in 1908 it received the grand name of 'Home Farm, East Twickenham'. In that year, Josiah Clarke, who had a milk business at 84 Hill Rise, Richmond (and also 18 children), moved his family to Park Lodge in Park Road and installed Jersey cows on his farmland opposite.

He also opened a dairy at the corner of Richmond and Morley Roads. The farmland was sold in 1920 after Clarke's death to Vickers for £1,000, who developed it as a sports ground. The dairy business still continued, as Hornby and Clarke, and the cows and farm moved to Petersham Meadows, across the river, and was later absorbed by Express Dairy. The actual dairy shop in Richmond Road, by then a self-service grocer's, closed in about 1970. Beresford Avenue was built on the sports ground in 1930.

182. *Twickenham Park under demolition, 1928, the site of Park House Gardens.*

183. *Whitton Village.*

The history of Park House Gardens was quite different. When the grounds of Twickenham Park were being broken up into smaller lots in the 1820s, a substantial house was built on a site about halfway down the Gardens; it eventually became known as Twickenham Park House. Its accompanying estate stretched to St Margaret's Road and comprised what are now Rosslyn Road, Riverdale Road and Gardens, Ellesmere Road, Arlington Road, Ravensbourne Road, The Barons, the Twickenham Film Studios and the small workshops in the old stables of the house beside the railway. Two lodges of this estate still survive at either end of Rosslyn Road.

By 1895 the large houses of Riverdale Road had been built, but it was not until the 1930s that the remainder of the roads mentioned above were completed. Twickenham Park House was demolished in 1929 and the surrounding land was excavated for gravel. In the early 1930s the gravel pit was filled in with, according to the local people, rubble and other material from the foundations of the old Hotel Cecil in the Strand. The first houses were then built in Park House Gardens at prices of up to £1600 for semi-detached houses with garages.

EXPANDING WHITTON

In the first ten years of the present century Whitton enjoyed a small building boom. Groups of terraced housing sprang up along Nelson, Hounslow and Kneller Roads, and there was also the building of Cedar Avenue, Seaton Road and Prospect Crescent. Two small parades of shops were built 1906-7 in Nelson Road and Hounslow Road to cater for the new residents. But the years of 1930-39 were to transform Whitton out of all recognition. Until the 1920s the village was separated from the surrounding towns by open fields and had a distinct identity; there was no railway station and the first bus service began only after the 1st World War.

The opening of Whitton railway station in 1930, however, hastened the demise of Whitton's isolation. In the 1930s virtually the whole of it was covered with three-bedroomed semi-detached houses, with some bungalows and a few larger houses. Houses around the station in roads such as Redway Drive and Constance Road were offered at between £700 and £900. Percy Road, between the Nelson and the railway bridge, a country lane in the 1920s, became the High Street in 1938.

There were also plans for civic buildings but it was not until the late 1950s that the land earmarked for these was used to build Whitton School, Heathfield Library, St Augustine's church and some local authority housing.

184. Chase Bridge.

185. Aerial view of Redway Estate, 1931.

One part that nearly escaped the 1930s unscathed was the Duke of Argyll's garden. A campaign was led by Alderman James Wills to keep this as a public park, but this failed and by 1937 it was under bricks and mortar. The final indignity was that one of the new roads was named after Alderman Wills.

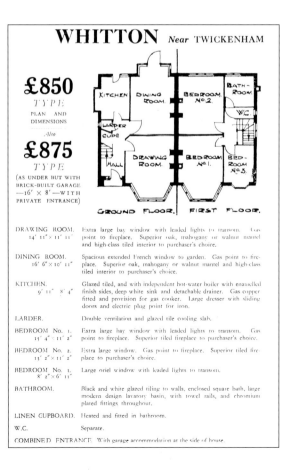

WHITTON *Near* TWICKENHAM

£850
TYPE
PLAN AND
DIMENSIONS
Also

£875
TYPE
(AS UNDER BUT WITH
BRICK-BUILT GARAGE
—16′ × 8′—WITH
PRIVATE ENTRANCE)

GROUND FLOOR.   FIRST FLOOR.

DRAWING ROOM.   Extra large bay window with leaded lights to transom.   Gas
14′ 11″ × 11′ 11′   point to fireplace.   Superior oak, mahogany or walnut mantel
and high-class tiled interior to purchaser's choice.

DINING ROOM.   Spacious extended French window to garden.   Gas point to fire-
16′ 6″ × 10′ 11″   place.   Superior oak, mahogany or walnut mantel and high-class
tiled interior to purchaser's choice.

KITCHEN.   Glazed tiled, and with independent hot-water boiler with enamelled
9′ 11″   8′ 4″   finish sides, deep white sink and detachable drainer.   Gas copper
fitted and provision for gas cooker.   Large dresser with sliding
doors and electric plug point for iron.

LARDER.   Double ventilation and glazed tile cooling slab.

BEDROOM No. 1.   Extra large bay window with leaded lights to transom.   Gas
15′ 4″ × 11′ 2″   point to fireplace.   Superior tiled fireplace to purchaser's choice.

BEDROOM No. 2.   Extra large window.   Gas point to fireplace.   Superior tiled fire-
13′ 2″ × 11′ 2″   place to purchaser's choice.

BEDROOM No. 3.   Large oriel window with leaded lights to transom.
8′ 2″ × 6′ 11″

BATHROOM.   Black and white glazed tiling to walls, enclosed square bath, large
modern design lavatory basin, with towel rails, and chromium
plated fittings throughout.

LINEN CUPBOARD.   Heated and fitted in bathroom.

W.C.   Separate.

COMBINED ENTRANCE.   With garage accommodation at the side of house.

186. Advertisement for Heathcote Estate.

Twickenham at War

CRIMEAN CONNECTIONS

There were several links between Twickenham and the Crimea. Tennyson, who wrote the *Charge of the Light Brigade*, had moved from Montpelier Row shortly before the war broke out. Lord Lucan, Cardigan's immediate superior at the Charge, had a sister who lived first at Orleans House and then at Cross Deep in the 1840s. James Searle who had been born in Twickenham and later moved to South Africa, where he became an MP, served in the Royal Navy in the Black Sea. Sgt Major Cole, who came to live in South Western Road at the turn of the century, joined the Rifle Brigade as a lad of 15, was wounded at Sebastopol and was nursed by Florence Nightingale.

The best-known Crimean connection was James Mustard. Born in 1829, he joined the 3rd Light Dragoons in 1852 where he was based at Hampton Court barracks before embarkation to the Crimea. He was with the Lancers at the famous Charge at Balaclava on 25 October 1854; he was slightly hurt but helped the wounded Trumpeter Landfried to safety. Out of 145 men in his regiment at the Charge only 38 survived.

His own brief account was recorded much later. 'All I know is that we started at a trot, then at a canter, and finally at a mad gallop in which horses and men were wedged together in one great mass. I was in the front rank. It was hell. Cannon belched forth shot and shell all round us and I saw many a comrade fall, but I got through all right. Then we turned. We came back in extended order but the ride was just as awful, just as maddening. I got a canister shot in my left side that cut my belt and sent my sword rattling to the ground.'

Mustard retired from the army ten years later with the rank of corporal and he married and settled in Twickenham, working as a tailor. At first he lived in Orleans Road but subsequently moved to 50 Winchester Road where he raised a family of four boys

187. Private James Mustard, 17th Lancers.

188. St Mary's church War Memorial. Wilfred Nevill's name is on the facing panel. (See next page).

and two girls. He was an early member of the Philanthropic Society and of the Ancient Order of Foresters. When he died in his 86th year in January 1916, the funeral service at St Mary's was with full military honours, and he now lies in the Twickenham municipal cemetery.

Another Twickenham resident who died in the Crimea lived at Heath House. There is a memorial to him in Holy Trinity church which reads: 'In memory of Lionel Daniel Mackinnon, Lieut. Colonel in the Coldstreams, Youngest son of W.A. Mackinnon M.P., He fell in action whilst gallantly leading on his men to repulse a very superior force of the enemy at the memorable Battle of Inkermann..'

BILLIE NEVILL'S FOOTBALLS

Some idea of the cost of the 1st World War can be gathered from the 120 names on the weathering cross in St Mary's churchyard, listing those who fell from what are now the parishes of St Mary's and All Hallows, many of them from well-known local families.

Some are just names, others we have details of. Thanks to the preservation of his letters, we know a good deal about Wilfred Percy Nevill, called Billie by his family. When he was nine years old he came to live with his family in Tennyson's old house in Montpelier Row in 1903. He sailed to France with the 8th Battalion of the East Surrey Regiment, and his elder sister, Amy, served with the Voluntary Aid Detachment in France and Italy. Fourteen days off his 22nd birthday, at 7.27am on 1st July 1916, Nevill led his B Company over the parapet of their trench into No Man's Land. During the night they had removed the barbed wire in front of their trenches, issued ammunition, sandbags, flares and tools and sufficient food to last each man 48 hours; they breakfasted at 4.30am including a rum ration, and at 6.30 the mist had lifted. One of his fellow officers later wrote: '...the company went over the top very well, with...your brother kicking off the company footballs.' By 7.50 the Battalion was in the first line of German trenches but Billie was killed just outside the German wire where both footballs were found the following day; they are now in the Regimental Museum. This was the first day of the Battle of the Somme - 19,000 were killed that day alone.

The story of the footballs was taken up by the press as an item of good news amongst such a disaster. The *Thames Valley Times* wrote, 'How the local men fought in the great advance' and 'Playing football under fire.'

"THE SURREYS PLAY THE GAME!" KICK

"ON THROUGH THE HAIL OF SLAUGHTER...THEY DRIVE T

189. *Men of the East Surrey Regiment following the football 1 July 1916. From the* Illustrated London News.

FOOTBALLS TOWARDS THE GERMAN TRENCHES UNDER A HAIL OF SHELLS.

DRAWN BY R. CATON WOODVILLE FROM MATERIAL SUPPLIED BY AN OFFICER PRESENT AT THE ACTION.

"RICKLING BALL": MEN OF THE EAST SURREYS CHARGING TOWARDS THE GERMAN TRENCHES AT CONTALMAISON.

190. *Review of Civil Defence Personnel at Fortescue House School by Admiral E.R. G.R. Evans ('Evans of the Broke'), Civil Defence Commissioner for London, 1941.*

191. *The ruins of Radnor House after bombing on 16 September 1940.*

TOTAL WAR 1939-1945

The casualties of the 2nd World War were not as grievous as in the 1st, but the conflict struck the locality in many ways. Numerous local people were involved in such services as the ARP and Civil Defence, the Home Guard, fire watching, and in reserved occupations for war work. Others took their boats to help in the exodus from Dunkirk in June 1940. Many were involved in 'digging for Victory', or else saved waste, sacrificed their house railings, endured food rationing and the cooking at 'British Restaurants', and took part in fundraising weeks which contributed to the purchase of two 'Twickenham' Spitfires. Although everyone had been issued with gas masks, as years passed fewer bothered to carry them.

Bombing in the Twickenham area began in August 1940 and for some months there were long night alerts, with civilians in Anderson or Morrison shelters. In September twelve people were killed and Radnor House was hit; sixteen were killed in October, and York House had to be evacuated because of an unexploded bomb. November brought the heavy total of 74 killed, more than sixty on the night of the 29th, when a major fire-bomb attack was followed by high explosives. The heaviest damage was in the Teddington area.

There was then a pause until June 1944 when the VI rockets came 'whiffling' through the skies. The fact that they were unmanned and so unpredictable when they cut out suddenly and glided to earth, did more to undermine morale than the more severe raids of 1940. Seventeen people died in June, all but one on the 19th when eight people were killed in Water Lane. The last fatality occurred on 29th August.

In all, thirty VI rockets fell on the Borough between 18 June and 29 August - the V2 rockets did not reach Twickenham. In this short period forty were killed and 110 were seriously injured. The total damage caused, chiefly in 1940 and 1944, included 497 houses destroyed, 1,872 badly damaged but repairable, and a further 30,000 slightly damaged. Throughout the Borough 144 (all but one civilians) were killed in air raids, the oldest 88, the youngest 7 weeks.

192. Whitton High Street after a VI hit on the night of 18/19 June 1944.

Old Houses find New Uses

YORK HOUSE AND THE 'NAKED LADIES'

Sir Ratan Tata, owner of York House, died in 1918 after several years of ill-health aggravated by hours in an open boat following the torpedoing of his ship en route from India two years earlier. When Lady Tata decided to return to India in 1922 their house was put on the market. At this time the Twickenham Urban District Council was keen to find a new home since the lease on the Town Hall in King Street had expired, and a strong pressure group was formed under the leadership of Noel Viner-Brady to urge the Council to acquire York House, rather than its proposed alternative, Richmond House, as a new town hall. The campaign succeeded and York House was formally opened as town hall by the Duke and Duchess of York on 16 November 1926, the year in which Twickenham became a borough.

York House continued to be the town hall of the enlarged Borough of Twickenham of 1937, and of the Greater London Borough of Richmond upon Thames

194. *Sir Ratan Tata and Lady Tata*

193. *York House*

195. *Statuary Group in York House Gardens. Photograph by Alan Urwin.*

from 1965, but it could by then only house a small portion of the Council's activities.

The statues of Carrara marble which are a striking feature of the riverside gardens of York House were brought to Twickenham in 1909 by Ratan Tata. They had been intended originally for Lea Park, the home of the financier, Whitaker Wright, but he, having been convicted of fraud, committed suicide by cyanide in 1904, and his property was sold off. The arrival of all this marble in Twickenham was not without incident: one consignment - a part of a dragon horse - fell off its horse-drawn cart just by St John's hospital, thereby injuring the cart, the horse and the hospital gate, though not the statue. The statues suffered a good deal over the years and major restoration work was undertaken in 1987-9 at a cost of some £55,000. This included replacing some fifty fingers, a horse's hoof, and some of the missing pearls, damaged or removed by vandals.

It is not known for certain who the original sculptor was, but contemporary reports (when the statuary came to Twickenham) speak of it as the work of an eminent Italian. What is known is that some other statues from Lea Park that have survived, were the work of O. Spalmach, then working in a Roman studio.

There is confusion as to what the group symbolises, although it is assumed that it must represent some tale from classical mythology. In 1914 the whole group was described as *Pegasus*, which is odd since there are two winged horses with a female rider. Since other figures in the group, described as nymphs, used to hold aloft pearls, the title *Pearl Fishers* has also been used. Because the female rider is standing on a shell, others have called the composition *The Birth of Venus* and yet others think the group represent the *Naiads*, but these are the nymphs of classical rivers and streams. If the group are nymphs, they are more certainly of the seas and oceans, and more properly should be called the *Oceanides*. However, the sensible folk of Twickenham avoid such abstruse problems and simply call them 'the Naked Ladies'.

196. *Orleans Gallery and the Octagon Room.*

ORLEANS HOUSE AND ITS GALLERY

After the death of William Cunard in 1906 there were several short-term occupants of Orleans House, but after the 1st World War it stood empty for several years. By 1926 it had been sold to the Crane River Sand and Ballast Co who demolished the greater part of the building before an adequate record of it could be made and dug out 200,000 tons of gravel from the site. Fortunately, the remainder, comprising the Octagon Room and adjacent wing, and the extensive stables behind, was purchased by the Hon. Mrs Walter Levey (later the Hon. Mrs Basil Ionides), daughter of Viscount Bearsted, who also bought the adjoining Riverside House. The land between the road and the river was eventually acquired by the Council for a public park and Mrs Ionides also contributed generously to that purchase. On the landward side, part of the grounds had been sold to the Eastern Telegraph Company to form the Exiles Sports Ground for their employees; Orleans Park School now occupies this site.

In 1962 Mrs Ionides died, bequeathing her riverside property and her large art collection of material of local interest to the Borough of Twickenham. The surviving portion of the main building of Orleans House was used at one stage as the exterior of Miss Havisham's Satis House in a television version of *Great Expectations*, but a more permanent use for it was its conversion into an art gallery, which was opened in 1972 and has been the venue for varied exhibitions, including the display of the Ionides collection and other items of local interest as well as more general topics. It now attracts some 20,000 visitors annually. The grounds, allowed to grow wild, form a peaceful haven which could be many miles from modern suburbia.

The Octagon Room forms part of the Gallery, and an Octagon Trust has been set up to research and reinstate some original features, and to redecorate the rich baroque interior in a way that Gibbs would have specified. A Twickenham Museum Group is endeavouring to raise money to establish a local history museum in part of the stable block.

INDEX
Illustrations in the text are noted by asterisks